D1559512

Jenny Lind

Jenny Lind, the "Swedish Nightingale."

Collector's Guide to Antique Paper Dolls

BY
CLARA HALLARD FAWCETT

with illustrations by the author

DOVER PUBLICATIONS, INC., NEW YORK

Published in Canada by General Publishing Company, Ltd.,
30 Lesmill Road, Don Mills, Toronto, Ontario.
Published in the United Kingdom by Constable and Company, Ltd.,
10 Orange Street, London WC2H 7EG.

This Dover edition, first published in 1989, is an unabridged
republication of *Paper Dolls: A Guide to Costume*, published by H. L.
Lindquist Publications, New York, in 1951. A new Publisher's Note has
been written specially for this edition.
    The publisher is grateful to The Corning Museum of Glass for
making the 1951 edition available for reproduction.

Manufactured in the United States of America
Dover Publications, Inc.
31 East 2nd Street
Mineola, N.Y. 11501

Library of Congress Cataloging-in-Publication Data

Fawcett, Clara Hallard.
[Paper dolls]
Collector's guide to antique paper dolls / by Clara Hallard
Fawcett ; with illustrations by the author.
p.   cm.
Reprint. Originally published: Paper dolls. New York, N.Y. :
H.L. Lindquist Publications, 1951.
Includes index.
ISBN 0-486-25956-0
1. Paper dolls—Collectors and collecting.   I. Title.
NK4893.F29   1989
769.5—dc19   88-32275
CIP

Dedicated to my friend
CAROL STEELE

Acknowledgment

I wish to express my grateful thanks to the many friends, collectors of paper dolls, who generously allowed me to copy from dolls in their collections in making my drawings. These include *Mrs. Dorothy Douse, Mrs. Jennie Calvert, Mrs. Beatrice McKenna, Mrs. Eleanor Childs*, all of Washington, D. C., *Miss Janet Pinney* of the Museum of the City of New York, *Mrs. Mary Mallon* of Philadelphia, *Miss Marian Howard* of Miami, Florida, *Mrs. Cora Lake* of Livingston, Montana and *Mrs. Willie Armstrong* of Austin, Texas.

CLARA HALLARD FAWCETT.

Publisher's Note

Within the last few years, paper dolls have become a popular collector's item. Most valuable, of course, are uncut sheets or books, complete with their original packaging. Paper dolls, however, were made to be played with, and dolls that have been cut out are much more readily available. With such sets, identification can be a problem, for often pieces are missing and the cover or envelope printed with the name and publisher of the set long since discarded.

In this book, Ms. Fawcett discusses scores of nineteenth- and early twentieth-century paper dolls. Although her original underlying intention was to encourage the use of paper dolls as a guide for making period doll clothing, her detailed descriptions and illustrations of the dolls and their costumes make the book a valuable reference for identifying these early paper dolls.

Contents

List of Illustrations

X

Chapter I

Paper Dolls, A Guide to Costume

PAPER dolls as a guide to costume had not occurred to Mrs. Sewso, a friend of the writer's, until one day when she decided to make an outfit for an old doll she had recently acquired—Matilda, a quaintly charming centenarian who had one thing in common with Lady Godiva when that gentle lady made her famous ride through Coventry. Mrs. Sewso pored over the contents of books on costume, but found them lacking in one important detail of a woman's toilette: they did not give enough attention to illustrations of underwear. Then it was suggested that she look over her large collection of old paper dolls. It seemed like an inspiration. The paper dolls not only furnished correct styles in underwear Melinda and her kind displayed in the secrecy of the boudoir, but many delightful and authentic ensembles in full color.

Collectors find discovery of antique paper dolls fully as exciting and interesting as unearthing real dolls, and when they are found, there is never the question: Is this dress original? It is not easy to locate old paper dolls, but if you make your wants known to friends and dealers, and especially if you are willing to advertise, the dolls will come to you. One of the finest collections in the country was built up through advertising for them.

It is surprising to find some sets of antique paper dolls in fresh, beautiful condition, but this often happens. Such a collection came to the writer because a mother of long ago thought the dolls much too pretty to be destroyed in play. The child was privileged only to look. How often children of the past were tantalized in this manner is evident by the number of real dolls in pristine condition that collectors in every state in the Union have been able to acquire. However, it must be remembered that the number of dolls broken and worn from use and cast into discard surely far exceeds the total salvaged for future generations to love and cherish.

The objection may be raised that we cannot obtain paper dolls old enough to represent fashions of many centuries ago, since paper dolls as fashion models did not appear until 1791. It is well to point out, however, that many hundreds of paper dolls in both the modern era and in bygone days have been made to represent earlier periods in history. Thus we have the lovely set of *Six Famous Queens and Martha Washington,* by E. S. Tucker, first published in the 1870's. In our own time there are *Dolls of Old Williamsburg* and *The Costume Party,* published by Samuel Gabriel Sons and Company of New York City. Besides these there are the hundreds of sets of paper dolls depicting stage and screen stars, representing real and fictional characters of long ago, presented in booklet form and distributed through the five-and-ten-cent stores throughout the country. If only the best of these had been saved for the last fifty years they would make a costume book second to none. Even the last ten or twelve years have given us a wealth of material in inexpensive booklet form. For instance, in one book alone, the *Jeanette Mac Donald Costume Parade Paint Book*, published in 1941 by the Merrill Publishing Company of Chicago, Illinois, forty-six costumes are shown in large clear sketches. These represent gowns used in Miss Mac Donald's various screen roles, such as *Romeo and Juliet* and *Naughty Marietta*. They demonstrate different periods of costume. In 1938 Shirley Temple, then a small child, posed for two paper dolls presented by the Saalfield Publishing Company of Akron, Ohio, and New York, N. Y. Accompanying the dolls were outfits she wore in her various screen roles, representing historical and national costumes as well as up-to-the-minute dresses of 1938. Such booklets as *Sonja Henie Hollywood Ice Show Dolls, Deanna Durbin Paper Dolls, Dionne Quints, Gone With the Wind, Dolls of All Nations*, and other similar ones, all published by Merrill, give interesting personalities as well as costumes. So also do the motion picture actresses produced by the Whitman Publishing Company of Racine, Wisconsin, and the Saalfield ones already mentioned. How many of us wish we had saved the paper doll book of the little English princesses, *Little Women*, when first this classic was put on the screen; and for costume, *Dresses Worn by the "First Ladies" of the White House*. In the latter the dolls themselves are not likenesses. The old magazine newspaper dolls of famous persons of not too long ago would be of interest. Our grandmothers and great grandmothers remember the paper dolls made to represent characters in *Uncle Tom's Cabin*, by Harriet Beecher Stowe; the marriage of General Tom Thumb, Eugenie of France, Victoria of England, and many other real and fictional persons who are dear to our memories. These dolls of yesterday, carelessly discarded by our forebears, are today highly treasured. Isn't it reasonable to expect that notables of today who have been represented in paper doll form will be just as highly treasured by our children's children in years to come?

Chapter II

A Brief History of Paper and Paper Dolls

THE history of paper dolls is necessarily associated with the history of paper. We know that the busy little wasp really was the first paper maker, but China is the country credited with its invention in commercial form. It is probable that the simple paper doll form was used soon after the invention of paper, which has been traced back to the second century B. C. Just as the real doll as a plaything came first to civilized countries, the same must have been true of the paper doll; and just as it is true that the real doll was first used for religious purposes, we may be sure this was the first purpose of the paper doll. Marco Polo described paper funeral images seen by him in China in the year 1280. They were used in ancient purification ceremonies. The idea was that if the paper doll were rubbed all over the body, then thrown into a river, one's sins would calmly float downstream and finally be lost at sea, leaving behind a pure and unstained soul. We wonder if girls and women had this soul-saving privilege, they were so little thought of at that time.

Few persons stop to reflect on how much of our civilization we owe to the manufacture of paper. Our knowledge of history, past and present, business transactions, and thousands of things too numerous to mention are dependent upon paper. The humble wasp little knew what a tremendous business he started when he showed us the material of which the vast majority of our paper still is made—wood pulp.

Captive Chinese were responsible for introducing paper-making to the outside world, winning their freedom in a Moslem country by working at their trade. These captives were instrumental in making Baghdad famous for paper-making, and from Baghdad the secret finally leaked out to the rest of the world. We have Arabic manuscript on paper dating back to the ninth century, which of course is much later than the invention of paper. It is thought that the Chinese at this period used bolls, reduced to pulp, from the cotton plant, while the Arabs and Persians resorted to flax from the papyrus plant. Oriental paper, in the middle ages, had a glossy surface without watermarks. The latter became universal in European factories. A quantity of our present-day paper is made from rags, but a still greater percentage is manufactured from wood pulp.

Until 1798 paper was handmade, but in that year Louis Robert, a clerk in a French paper mill, added immeasurably to the availability of the product by the invention of a machine for its manufacture. Henry Fourdrinier introduced a paper machine into England, and with the help of Bryan Donkin, achieved success in 1803.

A great many materials can be utilized in the manufacture of paper—the straw of wheat, oats, barley, rye, as well as rags and wood. The latter is used extensively by those countries which possess large forests. Spruce, Scotch fir, poplar, and aspen are preferred European sources, while in America we use hemlock and black spruce as well as poplar and aspen.

3

Wood can be disintegrated entirely by machinery, but the best method is by the use of chemicals. Since 1880 great advances have been made along this line. Paper-making machinery is complicated but fascinating. An interesting volume could be written on the subject. It has been responsible for the distribution of knowledge on a scale so vast as to be incalculable. Paper itself can be reduced to the pulp stage and re-assembled as papier mâché into many shapes and forms by pressing into molds while the sheets are still damp. For centuries many real dolls have been made in this way.

Paper figures and paper toys, some of them activated, were used in Europe as early as the fifteenth century. Figures were cut out and pinned together in

1.   Paper puppet c. 1835

Children playing with paper shadow puppet.

such a way that when they were placed over a hot stove, the rising heat would make them ''dance.'' The most interesting activated paper dolls were, of course, those with limbs and heads made separately, and hinged together by means of rods and strings, and made to act behind a lighted screen—our first motion pictures. (See sketch of children playing with a paper shadow puppet, No. 1. This is from a French woodcut of about 1835.)

Another idea for motion pictures, a simple affair, was worked out in the middle ages. A cardboard power wheel set in motion cardboard figures in the foreground of a shadow box. The power wheel was moved by sand poured from a tiny funnel at the back of the box, and this in turn moved levers which set the figures in motion. The popularity of this idea was revived in Europe in the eighteenth century, and in America between 1825 and 1875. Scenes from every-day life were depicted, such as a mother dangling her baby, and at the same time rocking back and forth in a chair.

Dean's Moveable Books published in London, England, in the early nineteenth century had motion pictures of a sort. Slots were cut in the incompleted picture through which the head and limbs appeared, the latter pasted on card-

2

2-a

3

Illustrations from Dean's book "Old Woman and Her Silver Penny."

board props, inserted through the back of the picture. By wiggling the main prop the heads and limbs were set in motion. See sketches.

Sketches 2 and 2-a show how the old woman in Dean's Book, "Old Woman and Her Silver Penny," made her head and arm move in unison with the head of the humorous ox, whose broad grin showed appreciation for the proffered water. Dotted lines in sketch No. 2 indicate the cut-away portion, and in No. 2-a they indicate the parts which are placed through the cutaway portions of sketch No. 2. The other sketch of the old woman shows her sweeping the floor, and it must have delighted children of long ago to see the broom actually move while the head of the lady nodded.

The drawings are reproduced through the courtesy of Mrs. Eleanor Childs of Washington, D. C.

A sketch takes up two-thirds of the page, and is followed by blank pages to keep the "works" in order. The story begins with the old woman sweeping her floor, and is followed by her choice of a little pig which she buys with a silver penny found in the dust of her sweepings. A wiggle of the prop at the foot of the picture enables the lady to pick up the smiling little piggie. Next is a stile which the animal refuses to cross, even though booted realistically as the woman's legs are made to move. Then, in turn, she appeals to a dog to bite the pig to make him cross, a stick to beat the dog, fire to burn the stick, water to quench the fire, an ox to drink the water, etc. All these things are uncooperative until finally a rat, by gnawing the rope which was meant to hang an obstinate butcher, sets everything in motion so that finally the old woman got her wish: "The pig soon leaped over the stile, and so the little old woman managed to get safely home with her pig that night; and a very fine pig it grew, I assure you."

Twenty-one series of books for children are advertised on the back covers of the book, including history, pastimes, plays, poems, nature lore, nursery stories, astronomy, geography, *Easy Guide to Useful Knowledge*, *Fourpenny School Books*, etc. One series that might be especially interesting is called *The Laughable Looking Glass for Little Folks*. The advertisement lists:

"Newman, one of the late writers in Punch. Humorous and abundant: Illustrations by H. McConnell. Price 2s. coloured, 1s. plain.

"This book, after the style of the German Struwellpeter, will indeed be found a rich treat for the little ladies and gentlemen of this present generation; and if some lesson from its teaching 'Serve to curb one passion wild, rich reward; for oh! 'tis something to have rightly taught a child!' "

Eleven stories are listed, with such titles as *Mischievous Fingers*, *Little Miss Consequence*, *The Conceited Child*, *The Little Slattern*. The advertisement concludes with the sentence, "These comical told tales to the above subjects are such that our Children will truly laugh and grow wise." *Spring Flowers and Summer Blossoms* is advertised "for the young and good."

Most of us are familiar with the paper Pantin which children in America call "jumping jack." The inspiration for this goes back to an early Egyptian toy doll which was activated by means of a thread attached to the loose limbs of the figure. It was introduced in Europe in 1662 in paper form called the Pantin, but did not reach the height of its perfection until 1746-1756. Favorites were

No. 4—from an Eighteenth Century Pantin.

Harlequin and Columbine. Elaborate and elegant costumes were made for the doll, and it became as much 'a craze with women of the eighteenth century as are dolls today. Finally it was prohibited by law in order, so it was thought, to protect expectant mothers who might, under the influence of the pantin's continual jumping, be in danger of bringing into the world children with twisted limbs. Later the pantin was revived, and still was being made in Germany up until the second World War. Sketch No. 4 is from an eighteenth century Pantin.

In the eighteenth century paper toys were very popular. German engravers made paper soldiers, all classes of the people, animals, houses, furniture, trees, flowers, grassy plots, theatres, picture galleries, every unit to make a complete town and to show the life of the people. These were pieced together to make whatever the child wished to portray—a village, a street scene, a furnished doll house, a peep-show, a company of parading soldiers, or what-have-you. Some of the best museums in this country and abroad have a fascinating record in the form of paper dolls and paper toys of the customs, manners, and costumes in full color of the past three hundred years.

It seems strange that paper dolls as we know them today, manikins with separate dresses and hats, or costume dolls, did not appear in Europe until 1791. at which time they were advertised in the *Journal der Moden* as follows:

"A new and very pretty invention is the so-called English doll which we have lately received from London. It is properly a toy for little girls, but is so pleasing and tasteful that mothers and grown women will likely also want to play with it, the more since good and bad taste in dress or coiffure can be observed and, so to speak, studied. The doll is a young female figure cut out of stout cardboard. It is about eight inches high, has simply curled hair, and is dressed in underclothing and corset. With it go six complete sets of tastefully designed dresses and head-dresses which are cut out of paper. . . . The whole thing comes in a neat paper envelope which can be easily carried in a hand-bag or work-box to give amusement at parties or to children."

The custom of presenting paper dolls in "a neat paper envelope" continued for many years thereafter. Some examples are given in the pages which follow.

One of the most interesting ideas for paper dolls was introduced by England in the early 1800's. Paper dolls representing characters in a book were placed in a pocket at the back of the volume. About 1806 S. & J. Fuller of London brought out some of these books written by Dr. Walcott entitled *Little Henry, Phoebe the Cottage Maid,* and *Lauretta the Little Savoyard.* There were many others. The object of children's literature of the period seems to have been to impress upon small minds the dire consequences of naughtiness and the rich rewards of virtue.

In an interesting article written by Miss Marian B. Howard of Miami, Florida, it is stated:

"In 1814 a Cinderella cutout book appeared, Cinderella's head made to slip into openings in different settings, including her coach window. The present day JUDY AND JIM cutout book has this same feature, the paper dolls fitting into slots cut in garden paths, near the Christmas tree, in their little beds, etc. There is a wardrobe in which their costumes can be slipped.

"In 1819 a French story of Annette came out, with Annette in paper doll form. together with three changes of custome, enclosed in an envelope which was glued inside the back cover of the book. Today we find similarity in the ME AND MIMI book brought out by Samuel Lowe Company in 1942. Big Me is the large featured cutout doll, while Little Me with three changes of costumes, enclosed in an envelope which was glued inside the back cover the larger book."

Miss Howard goes on to tell of another 1941 Samuel Lowe book. She says:

"This is a Three-in-one—three books of varying sizes roped together and a carrying handle, striped like a barber pole, provided. The top and smallest book features The Five Little Peppers; the middle sized one Little Women, and the bottom and longest book is Annie Laurie in corset and underskirt with eight beautiful Godey type costumes and many accessories, such as gloves, fans, fur neck pieces, extra collars, etc."

Many old ideas for paper dolls are in use today. For instance, the principle of our "round-about" or three dimensional paper doll was figured out a hundred and fifty years ago; our "pop-up" book was offered for sale in 1840 under the title, *The Surprise Picture Book.* (See Sketch No. 5.) A copy of this book may be seen in the Stuttgart Landesgewerbe Museum, Germany. The principle of one of our twentieth century "walking" paper dolls was patented, in a different costume, of course, in 1874 by William H. Hart, Jr., of Philadelphia. This is referred to in a later chapter.

In other countries, too, old ideas survive. In China the paper Kitchen God, Tsao Chün, still holds its place. Elsie Clark Krug of Baltimore writes:

"He is a sort of secret police for the supreme Taoist Deity. This Kitchen God is simply a picture of Tsao Chün on a piece of red paper. It shows him as a bewhiskered observer surrounded by a group of children or attendants, and one of the ceremonies of the New Year in millions of homes in China is the fastening up of a new Kitchen-god on the wall of the brick stove. He serves as a visible conscience, as his duty is to observe all the family doings and report on their behavior. A family that is very careful will show him special

5.

The Surprise Book of about 1840.

attention twice a month, at new and full moon. The careless will try to make up for their negligence by smearing honey on his mouth on New Year's Eve when he goes up to the Taoist heaven to make his annual report. The honey will make him say sweet things, or at least will keep him from reporting too much that might be detrimental to his appeasers on earth.

"Chinese kitchens are smoky, and by the end of twelve months Tsao Chün's visage is covered with grime. So in the general cleaning for the New Year the old picture is taken down and burned (to help him go up in smoke to the upper regions) and a new picture is pasted up."

It would take a large-sized volume merely to skirt the subject of the paper doll as a cutout and as an activated toy, for the period covers many hundreds of years. The purpose of this book, however, is mainly to deal with the paper doll as we know it, the costume doll, a comparatively recent invention, as we have pointed out. It is hoped that the reader will find ideas for dressing antique and costume dolls, as well as for theatrical and party costumes, and that the collector of paper dolls will add to his store of knowledge of that fascinating hobby.

Chapter III

Early Paper Dolls

PAPER dolls made before the mid-nineteenth century are difficult to find. Mr. Wilbur Macey Stone, in a booklet published in 1932 in connection with an exhibit of paper dolls at the Newark, New Jersey, Museum, tells of "two early examples, credited to about 1700," but they are not paper dolls with separate dresses.

The earliest costume paper doll the writer has seen is French, dated 1822. It may be seen at the Museum of the City of New York. (See Illustration No. 6.) Sketches of the doll, No. 7 with her seven dresses and six hats, are shown here through the courtesy of the Museum. The set formerly belonged to Mrs. Benjamin Welles, grandmother of the donor, Miss Georgiana A. Sargent.

The dress shown on the doll has a pale yellow background with vari colored flower design, white trimmings at neck, sleeve, flounce, and sash.

The outfit at the left of the doll consists of a blue dress with yellow at the edges of the trimming, and a yellow hat with plumes and ribbon trimming, the latter in stripes of red and green.

The costume at the extreme right of the doll consists of a blue and yellow plaid cape, lined with pink to match the pink dress, and a pink hat.

The central costume in the upper row is a study in white, yellow, and lavender.

The center dress in the lower row is white with a tan scarf, the latter trimmed with deeper tan and yellow stripes. The hat is yellow, with white and green ribbon trimming. The outfit at the left of this is pink, accompanied by a yellow scarf and pink hat, and the dress at right is light yellow with scarf and hat of red with black and gold stripes.

Playing with paper dolls was a pastime for grown up young ladies as well as children of the early 1830's, judging from an old French woodcut. (See Sketch No. 8.) This shows a group of females past their childhood grouped around a table on which is a box of paper dolls. A doll stands on the table, and each of two ladies holds a paper doll dress. They all wear the quaint costume with wide sleeves and elaborate hairdo fashionable in 1828-1833. The woodcut is unsigned.

Not many paper dolls of the 1830's have turned up in collections, but the Museum of the City of New York has a charming nine-inch handmade, hand-colored doll of this period, the gift of Miss Constance Kilbourn, whose great, great grandmother was the artist. The doll, a brunette, and two of her seven dresses are sketched here through the courtesy of the Museum. (No. 9) The pose would suggest a ballet dancer, but the dresses are typically peasant. That at upper left of the doll consists of a dark bodice trimmed at the neck with green and yellow material; white puffed sleeves, an upper skirt of red with

A French costume paper doll, dated 1822, the earliest author has seen.
It is in the Museum of the City of New York. Her seven dresses and
six hats are shown on page 12.

7

Costumes of 1822 French doll shown on page 11.

8   c. 1830

Old French woodcut showing young women playing with paper dolls, circa 1830.

yellow and white trimming, and a dark green underskirt with yellow trimming.

The costume at lower left consists of a black bodice, white puffed sleeves with blue bows on the shoulders, and a blue skirt with white trimming. The apron also is white.

The first of the really old dolls to come to the writer's attention, was owned by Mrs. Jennie Calvert of Washington, D. C., who at that time was president of the Colonial Dames, a patriotic organization. She had asked the writer to talk on dolls at a meeting of the Club, and afterward spoke of these paper dolls that she had inherited. "My mother would not allow me to play with the dolls," said Mrs. Calvert, "for fear I would spoil them, and I guess Mother herself did not play with them much, for they are in fine condition in spite of the fact that they are nearly a hundred years old." Two of the dolls are illustrated in an earlier book, *Dolls—A Guide for Collectors*,* but there is so much interest in them that it is thought best to reproduce the whole set. This consists of two boys exactly alike, with six costumes, including hats; two girls alike except for the hair ribbon, which on one is red, on the other blue; (the girls also have six costumes including hats) and two ladies with nine dresses and nine hats between them. They are beautifully printed both back and front in full color. All have blue eyes and light brown hair. The "children" are four inches tall, and their "mammas" six and one-half inches in height. The names given are for convenience.

"John" (Sketch No. 10) wears a pair of tightly fitting tan trousers, blue jacket with gold buttons, and a white blouse showing underneath. Tie and slippers are red. His "little-boy" costume (10-a) is a green, yellow, blue, and red plaid, with orange banding; white blouse and pantalettes; green shoes. A tan basket of ferns and purple fruit is held in one hand. The red cap with black visor has a yellow, and green plaid band with yellow buckle and tassel.

---

*Written by Ms. Fawcett, now out of print.

Brunette doll, with two of her seven dresses, circa 1830, in the Museum of the City of
New York, and shown through their courtesy.

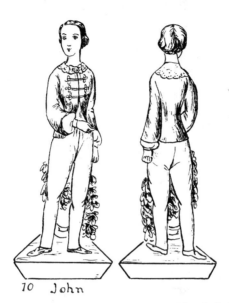

10 John

John, with his tight-fitting tan trousers, blue jacket with
gold buttons, and a white blouse showing underneath.
His tie and slippers are red.

10-a

John's garden costume of green, yellow, blue, and red plaid, with
orange banding. The blouse and pantelettes are white; the shoes,
green. He carries a tan basket of ferns and purple fruit.

10-b

10-c

John's hunting outfits.

No. 10-b is a "play hunting" outfit. A short red dress with white collar shows underneath a green hunting jacket with a front inset of black to match the design around the bottom of the red skirt. Boots are gray, cap green with a black band, stockings white and the dog tan. Pantalettes accompanying all the costumes for both boy and girl are white.

No. 10-c is another hunting costume. The overblouse is red with white dots, there is a black band at neckline, white at throat and sleeve edges, and the skirt is green. Long gaiters are black, and the cap is plum colored, trimmed with a yellow band and gray feathers. The figure stands on a yellow ground with a gray stone to the rear.

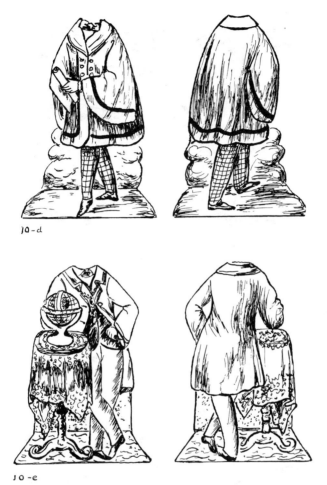

John's graduation costume, at top; student's costume, below.

Judging from the scroll, No. 10-d is a graduation costume. It consists of a brown coat and green checked trousers, blue tie and black shoes. A snowy background would indicate a mid-winter graduation. Evidently the little fellow is growing up without adding height to his years.

No. 10-e is a student's costume with greenish-blue trousers, blue tie, white shirt, black vest and tan overcoat. The background of the tablecover is red with designs in yellow, and the carpet yellow with green designs.

No. 10-f is meant for a costume party. The coat is red, shaded parts in the sketch blue, and the frogs are yellow matching the pants. Stockings and vest are white, and the slippers black with yellow buckles. The figure is standing on a green base and leaning on a gray slab.

Costume 11-a consists of a plum-colored coat trimmed with ermine, and a green dress trimmed with black braid. Ribbons hanging from a gray hat match the coat, and the feathers match the white ermine trimming. A coat of egg white

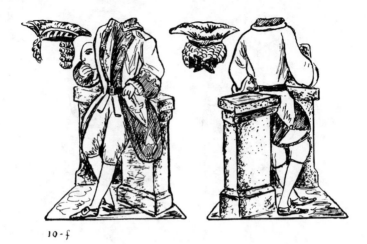

10-f

John's masquerade party outfit.

applied long ago has softened all the colors of the children's costumes, so that pristine whiteness has turned a soft yellow. The dolls themselves are not so coated; neither are the lady dolls nor their clothes.

An outfit for school is shown in sketch 11-b. The coat is blue with black trimming and gold buttons and with a white lace collar and white sleeves making a contrast. A yellow skirt has a deep orange leaf design which matches the book binding. Red flowers and white ruching relieve the dark blue bonnet, and a dash of blue-green on the page of the open book matches the high gaiters.

No. 11-c is a garden outfit in gay yellow with red ribbons down the skirt, interrupted by pleats of the same material as the skirt. It is relieved by a black lace fichu-basque. A yellow straw hat has green ribbon trimming, and the shoes are gray. A basket of fruit is held in one hand.

"Mary and her little lamb" appear in sketch 11-d. The dress is yellow with deeper yellow stripes, and has a puffy overdress in deep orange trimmed with blue ribbon to match the edge of the black cape-sleeve jacket basque. A white blouse is trimmed with green ribbons at the sleeves, and a stick tied with a pink bow is seen over one shoulder. A blue flower arrangement for the hair completes the costume. Mary's lamb is white.

Costume 11-e consists of a brown basque with white collar and undersleeves, and a cerise skirt. The figure stands on a yellow carpet with designs in green, and carries a white "bunny."

The masquerade party costume, 11-f is a truly magnificent affair. It consists of an elaborate white lace ruffled skirt and sleeves, the latter barely showing underneath a red velvet overdress with gold trimming. A green fan matches the color of the bows on the yellow vest.

The "ladies" remind one of the Jenny Lind doll, published in 1850, for they are of the same general style, with the hair slicked back to allow for an extra wig. The women each have four costumes with the addition of a long bridal veil and an extra wig for "Jenny." Light brown shoes match the hair in each

Mary, a paper doll of the 1850's.

Mary's winter outfit, a plum-colored coat trimmed with ermine, and gray hat trimmed with feathers.

11-b

11-c

Mary's school outfit is shown at the top. Coat is blue, with white lace collar and white sleeves making contrast. In the bottom sketch we see Mary's garden outfit in a gay yellow with red ribbons.

11 d

11-e

11-f

Nursery Rhyme outfit, Mary and lamb, at top; center play dress of brown basque and cerise skirt; bottom, masquerade party costume.

12

Jenny

Jenny, like the other lady dolls, has four costumes, but she has in addition
a bridal veil and an extra wig. She dates in the 1850's.

Jenny-a

Jenny's formal frock of white with a little pink flower design. She has
yellow gloves, carries a white handkerchief, and wears a gold bracelet.

case. Differences in the two are in the pose, the arrangement of the knot at
the back of the head, the cut of the bodice of the underwear, and the color of
the carpet on which they stand. The carpet under Jenny is light plum, under
her twin, light pink, and the shoes of the latter are a darker tan. Jenny's separate wig is decorated with blue bows, four of them, evenly spaced around the
hair.

The costume marked *Jenny-a,* a formal frock, is white with a little pink
flower design, and pink ribbons, and there is a tiny scalloped edge in pink around
the collar, edges of the filmy overdress and sleeve ruffles. Accessories are
yellow gloves, gold bracelet and a white handkerchief.

Jenny-b seems to be a bridal outfit, the bonnet to be worn on other occasions,
perhaps, with the same dress. The skirt has five flounces of lace, and there are
ruffles of lace with ruching on the waist and elaborate sleeves. In the hand
is a pretty bouquet of red and yellow flowers, and there is a corsage of the same
posies. The brim of a yellow bonnet is edged with pale blue lace, and white
plumes adorn the back of the headgear. Tiny red roses are seen on either side of
the lower edge of the brim, and the tie is pale blue. The white bridal veil illustrated is crowned with a wreath of yellow flowers and green leaves.

An elegant red jacket trimmed with ermine, and a green two-flounced skirt
with a fine design in black is labelled *Jenny-c.* There are yellow tassels hanging
from the waist, and the sleeve showing underneath the sleeve of the jacket is
white, shaded in blue, which matches a tiny ruffle at the neck. The hat is gray
trimmed with a pale blue plume and green ribbons.

Jenny-b

Jenny's costume above appears to be a bridal outfit.

Jenny-c

An elegant red jacket trimmed with ermine for Jenny to wear in winter.

Jenny-e

Jenny's Bridal Veil.

Jenny - d

Jenny's riding outfit.

The riding outfit, *d*, must have been most uncomfortable in mounting and riding a horse. The figure holds up a green skirt high enough to reveal a dainty white lace-edged petticoat. The jacket is cream color, although it might have been white originally, and there is a red bow at the neck. Gloves are light gray, and the riding whip black with a gold-edged handle.

Matilda's formal costume *a* is one of the loveliest of the set. The background color is warm light brown with white diamond striped bands enlivened with a pink flower in the center of each diamond running down the length of the skirt both back and front. On either side of the front of the skirt is a straight panel of black velvet decorated with rows of white ruffling, matching the yoke of the bodice, and on either side of the yoke is a curved panel of black velvet, which continues more than half way down the front of the costume, held in place at the waist by a black velvet bow. A white scalloped edge on the black velvet trimmings adds to the effectiveness. Under the divided sleeve cape, the latter also edged with white, is a white puffed short sleeve. Accessories are gold bracelets, white gloves and handkerchief.

Costume *b*, a walking outfit, is pink with green plaid stripes, white sleeves to match shirring at the neckline of the bodice and pink bands of shirring divide the puffs of the sleeves. The hat is pink with white trimming on crown and brim. A pink ribbon band at the neck, gold bracelets, pale cream gloves, a green fan and white handkerchief add finishing touches.

13.

Matilda

Front and rear view of Matilda.

Matilda - a

Matilda's lovely formal costume.

Matilda - b

A walking outfit for Matilda.

Matilda-c

A Sunday walking, or calling outfit for Matilda.

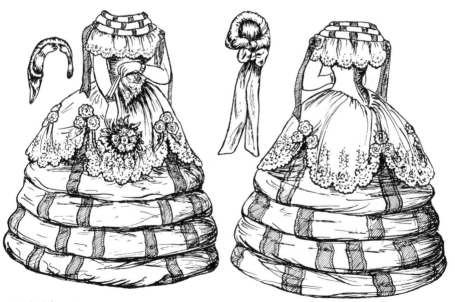

Matilda-d

Matilda's white party dress.

Matilda's costume c, although very elaborate, seems to be a calling or a walking outfit, judging from the little white sunshade carried in one hand. Perhaps it was meant for a Sunday afternoon. The dress is blue with gold buttons down the front of the basque. The color is relieved by large white ruffled lace sleeves and a plain lace collar. Sash and bows on the sleeves are pink. Headgear is gray overlaid with white ostrich feathers and trimmed with red flowers and green leaves.

Matilda's white party dress, d, reminds one of a wedding cake with its wide skirt in rolls like layers of a cake. It is trimmed with pink "candy stripe" ribbon, and the lace pannier is caught up with pink posies. The figure wears cream colored gloves and carries a blue fan and white handkerchief in one hand, in the other a bouquet of pink flowers with a center flower of yellow, contrasting nicely with the encircling green leaves. The bracelets are gold, and a fine line of gold edges the fan. Hair ribbons in the separate wig are pink.

"Nora," No. 14, published about the middle of the last century, is one of the most interesting paper dolls in the writer's own collection. It follows the pattern of most of the American paper dolls of this period in that it is uncolored except for tinting of flesh, hair and shoes. Costumes, however, are colored. Nora's hair and shoes are light tan, and she wears a pink hair ribbon. This doll and her clothes, unlike those just described, are printed on one side only. Plain paper is attached to the reverse side, but only a little more than half way down, and the sides are pasted together at the edges so that the costume may be slipped on over the head.

The afternoon dress at the left of the doll is a white dotted Swiss with blue bands on the skirt and blue shirring on the bodice and sleeves. Big white undersleeves are edged with lace. The fan is yellow with red at the base.

The background material of the walking costume at the right of the figure is white with stripes in dark blue, yellow, red and light green. The dress is accompanied by an ermine stole and muff, the latter with dark blue tassels. Undersleeves are white.

The Sunday dress at the extreme left, lower row, is pink with black squared lines, and white ruching edges the oversleeve, stole and neckline, matching the white undersleeves. Mitts are black.

The center costume, lower row, is milady's riding habit. It consists of a blue jacket with lower edge of gold color, matching the gloves. The skirt is foliage green.

The party costume at extreme right, lower row, is white trimmed with yellow ruching, over an underskirt of pale lavender. Roses decorating the dress are red with encircling green leaves.

In the course of collecting dolls, real or paper, many unidentified ones come to hand, but often we can judge of the period by clothing, and by comparison with known dolls of the same general type. Miss Marian Howard of Miami, Florida, has a delightful boy paper doll which Harriet Tucker, the person from whom Miss Howard received the doll, claims to be more than one hundred years old. There were three early American publishers of paper dolls who are fairly well known to collectors: the dolls of McLoughlin Brothers;

Nora and her various costumes: afternoon dress (a); walking costume (b); Sunday dress (c); riding outfit (d); party dress (e).

Chandler's dolls, published for Brown, Taggard and Chase of Boston; and the dolls of Clark, Austin and Smith of New York City. These firms seem to have done a flourishing business in this line as early as the 1850's. McLoughlin Brothers, Inc., of Springfield, Massachusetts, formerly of New York City, started in business in 1828, but since all their early records were destroyed by flood some years ago, they have no knowledge of just what year their publications included paper dolls. However, Miss Howard's little boy paper doll resembles a Clark, Austin and Smith doll rather than McLoughlin's. It is possible that Chandler designed it, although it does not fit in with the six known Chandler dolls. Again, it might have been published by an unknown firm with a style similar to Clark, Austin and Smith.

The boy referred to (No. 15), named Howard after the present owner, is dressed in long white underwear, as shown in the sketch. Costume *a* consists of a

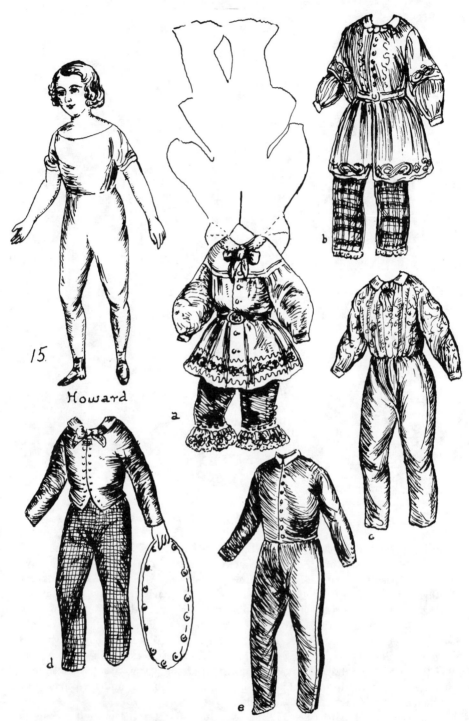

15.

Howard

Howard and his costumes: Dress-up (a); semi-dress-up (b);
play (c and d); school costume (e).

Above, Fanny Fair and formal dress. Below, Dorothy and her plaid every-day dress.

18.

Eva

19.   Emma

Eva and Emma are unidentified dolls in the collection of Mrs. Dorothy Douse of Washington, D. C. They came in the same group, and their names were in pencil on the back of the dolls.

Charley, an 1857 doll, and the original envelope in which he came.
Every-day jackets (a and b); every-day outfit (c); walking
costume (d).

pink overdress with white collar, deeper pink tie and trimming around skirt, dark blue belt and trousers, the latter edged with white lace ruffles. We wonder how a six-year-old boy of today would like the outfit!

Sketch *b* shows the same general style, but is less fancy. The overdress is yellow with white collar and sleeves, pink belt and green plaid trousers edged with white embroidery.

Costume *c* consists of an all-pink blouse and tan pants; *d*, a green jacket with white collar and tie and gray checked trousers; *e* is pale green with a white collar and epaulets.

"Fanny Fair" (No. 16) is an uncut paper doll with no identification except the printed name at the right side of the card. She is from the fine collection of Mrs. Dorothy Douse of Washington, D. C. "Fanny" is flesh-tinted by hand and in her hair is a pink rose. She has embroidered white underwear, and the pantalettes end in wide lace ruffles. At the right of the doll is a white afternoon or formal dress embroidered in pink, and there are red bows on the sleeves.

"Dorothy" (No. 17), named after her present owner, Mrs. Douse, stands on a red stool with green fringe. She also is flesh-tinted and has light brown hair. Her dress is uncolored except for a strip of red over the design in the upper skirt, and, in like manner, green on the under skirt. Her separate costume is white with red plaid stripes.

Mrs. Douse has many charming early unidentified paper dolls, such as "Eva" (No. 18). The name was written in pencil on the back of the doll, probably by the first small owner, and is not the commercial appendage. "Eva" came with many dainty costumes made or cut out by hand, the little owner of long ago using decorated paper in the quaint and pretty designs of her time. Some of these dresses have dates on the back, in one instance 1851, in another, 1853. Included are boy and women paper dolls in attractive poses.

21   Little Fairy Lightfoot

Little Fairy Lightfoot and two of her dresses.

Goody Two-Shoes and envelope in which she came. Plaid dress (a);
dress with sack (b); every-day dress (c); afternoon frock (d).

Another doll which came in the same group is "Emma" (No. 19). The name is pencilled on the back. She has a green bow and red posies in her hair, and is on a green standard. Dolls 16-19 probably are McLoughlin dolls.

Mrs. Douse also has some of the Chandler paper dolls, of which Mr. Herbert H. Hosmer, Jr., of South Lancaster, Massachusetts, speaks in his illustrated leaflet. "Charley" (No. 20) came complete with costumes and in his original envelope, reproduced here through the courtesy of Mrs. Douse. Very fine printing on the bottom of the envelope reads: "J. G. Chandler, W. Roxbury, Mass. Entered according to act of Congress in the year 1857 by J. G. Chandler in the Clerk's office of the District Court of Mass." It will be noted, from the flap of the envelope, that there are six dolls in this series, No. 1, Carry; No. 2, Alice; No. 3, Charley; No. 4, Little Fairy Lightfoot; No. 5, Betty, the Milkmaid and All Her Pets; and No. 6, Jack and His Holiday Companions.

Mr. Hosmer has reproduced a leaflet containing two of the Chandler dolls and their outfits, Little Fairy Lightfoot (No. 21) and Charley (the latter he has renamed Jack) and sells it either colored or uncolored, whichever you prefer.

Goody Two-Shoes (No. 22) and the envelope in which she came, published by R. A. Hobbs of Lowell, Massachusetts, also found their way to the home of Mrs. Douse, through whose courtesy the doll and envelope are reproduced.

The envelope has some touches of color. The hair of the figure is brown, sash and shoes, Lake-red, and the trimming around neck and skirt-band yellow ochre. There is also a touch of yellow ochre under the feet of the doll on the cover. The doll itself is uncolored except for hair and shoes, which are the same as the figure on the envelope.

The plaid dress marked *a* has red eyelet embroidery at neck and sleeves, and is gaily trimmed with Lake red ribbon; otherwise the dress is uncolored.

In sketch *b* we have a yellow sack trimmed with Lake red to match the red band on a green skirt.

Sketch *c* is a yellow dress with white trimming at neck and sleeves. The sash is red at the waist line, but one streamer only is red, the other green, exactly like the sash in sketch *d*. In the latter, the dress is neutral yellow, as though aged that color. Flowers in the band around the skirt are red.

Another of the paper dolls which came in a "neat paper envelope" is "Miss Florence" (No. 23), illustrated here together with the envelope in which she came. The doll itself is reproduced through the courtesy of Mrs. Douse. The writer has the envelope and five costumes.

Two copies of the dress marked *a* came in the envelope, one colored and one uncolored, and one with lace pantalettes, the other without, as sketched. The leaf designs in the scallops on either side of the panel and around the bottom of the skirt are embroidered alternately in red and blue, and the insertion in the panel down the center of the dress is embroidered in blue. *b* is a red plaid with trimmings of darker red moire ribbon; collar and sleeve ruffles, white lace. The two-flounced dress, *c*, is white lace with white braid trimming on the bodice. *d* is canary yellow with yellow scalloped ruffles edged with two bands of blue, which, in turn, are edged with white. A blue bow at the neck completes the costume. Printing on the envelope for Miss Florence reads as shown under illustration on page 39.

THE GIRLS' DELIGHT.

PAPER DOLLS—NUMBER ONE.

Miss Florence--with her wardrobe complete--a delightful and elegant amusement for litt[...]rls.

23.

"The Girls' Delight. Paper Dolls—Number One. Miss Florence—with her wardrobe complete—a delightful and elegant amusement for little girls. We presume all our young lady friends will see very readily how to prepare Miss Florence, her dresses, &c. If, however, any should be puzzled at all about the right way to do it, a beautiful little book called 'Paper Dolls and How to make them,' will tell them all about it. If you cut around the hands and arms, where they are joined to the body, and bring them in front of her dress, it will improve the effect. One dress is left plain so that it may be colored according to taste . . . Clark, Austin & Smith."

Miss Florence, and below, transcription of printed matter on her envelope. Party dress (a); every-day dress (b); afternoon costume and frock (c and d).

Miss Hattie

Miss Hattie, the second in the series of Clark, Austin and Smith dolls. Party dress (a); every-day dress (b and c); afternoon frock (d and e); bonnet (f); cape (g); Sunday dress (h).

Again the writer is indebted to Mrs. Douse for the privilege of reproducing ""Miss Hattie"" (No. 24), the second in the series of Clark, Austin and Smith dolls, and the text on the envelope, which reads:

"The Girls' Delight. Paper Dolls—Number Two. A delightful and elegant amusement for little girls.
"Miss Hattie—with dresses, &c., for all occasions. A dress for morning and one for evening, one for a walk with a bonnet and cape, one for school and one· for her birthday party. All who have had number one (Florence) will understand how to prepare Hattie, her dresses, &c. Those who have not, will learn all about it from a beautiful little book called 'Paper Dolls and How to make them.' As the sleeves of the two blue dresses *lap* onto the dress, you must cut little slits with a sharp pointed knife, just below the undersleeve, large enough for the hand and arm to go through. Be careful not to cut to the outside of the dress, and also be careful to follow the line of the *lower* edge of the white undersleeve. Put the hands through these slits *before* putting the dress over the head, then cut a piece from the back of the dress close to the neck as large as the head and put the head through the opening thus made, and bring down the dress to its proper place, and Miss Hattie will look well enough to go to her sister's wedding.
"Clark, Austin & Smith, 3 Park Row, N. Y."

The dresses are colored as follows: *a*, yellow with blue trimmings and sash; *b*, white dots on a blue background; wine colored ribbon; white undersleeves showing; orange-pink edging on revers and sleeve ruffles, with matching sash: *c*, blue and white stripes with red bands on sleeves, at neckline, and a red sash; white undersleeves showing: *d*, blue bodice with white trimming, red. overskirt, yellow lace underskirt: *e*, yellow background with green stripes, pink and red trimming, pink bows on sleeves and pink sash: *f*, green bonnet with red flowers and plaid ribbon; white ostrich plumes: *g*, green with pink ribbons.

One of the most interesting sets of paper dolls published by Kimel and Forster of New York City about 1866 was called "The American Lady and her Children in a Variety of the Latest Beautiful Costumes." There were twenty-five changes. Backs and fronts of dresses were glued together at the edges and slipped on over the head of the doll.

The booklet referred to on the Clark, Austin & Smith paper doll envelopes was the second edition of "Paper Dolls and How to Make Them," published by D. F. Randolph of New York City. He also published the same year "The Paper Doll Family" with seven figures and costumes. The former had long intrigued the writer's curiosity when she happened to come across a copy through attending an auction of old books, papers and manuscripts. After winning a bid on children's books, and giving her name, a gentleman sitting near ventured to say, "You don't happen to be Clara Hallard Fawcett, author of books on dolls, do you?" In the course of the ensuing conversion, in which mutual interests were revealed, it was disclosed that the gentleman, Mr. John M. Connor of Plainfield, New Jersey, had in his possession a copy of the booklet in question. Through his courtesy it is given in toto in the following chapter.

Chapter IV

"Paper Dolls and How to Make Them,"

A Booklet of 1857

THE booklet referred to in the previous chapter, *Paper Dolls and How to Make Them,* was published by Anson D. F. Randolph of New York City In itself the booklet is not impressive, but it was important in stimulating interest in homemade paper dolls in the eighteen fifties. Collectors often come across individual dolls either cut or copied from the little book, but do not know their source. It is for this reason that the complete booklet and its illustrations are given in this chapter. Judging from some of the sketches the artist knew little about the human form divine, but the head of each figure is fairly well drawn. Plate I, No. 26, reminds one of Alice in Wonderland when she first started to grow. The faces are very lightly tinted with flesh color; hair and shoes are light tan. The dolls in all the plates have the same coloring, except for footwear, which varies slightly.

Plate II, No. 27, consists of four dresses and a hat. The dress marked *a* is light tan with red cuffs and trimming, gray belt, white collar; *b* is medium blue with white ruffles at cuffs, and directly above is a white hat with pink bow and white plume; *c* is a white dress with criss-crosses in pink, white apron; *d* consists of a white upper with a foliage green skirt.

The doll in Plate III, No. 28, is tinted exactly like the startling young creatures in Plate I except that the slippers are sky blue, the same color as the ribbons in the white hat and the little sack. The latter is bound in white.

2 5.

Cut-outs made from folded paper.

PLATE I.

26.

Plate I, reminiscent of Alice in Wonderland when she started to grow.

PLATE II

27.

Plate II, consisting of four dresses and a hat.

Plate III, with doll tinted like those in Plate I.

Separate shoes and stockings are pink stockings, tan shoes. The separate dress with apron is pink and white striped, pink sash, white apron, the chemise and sack white, the latter belted with pink ribbon, and the cape is red with red criss-cross stripes on the white trimming.

In Plate IV, No. 29, the sack at left of the figure is white with a blue belt; the one at right is red with darker trimming. In the lower left-hand side of the plate is a cape and leggings outfit of light tan with darker trimming, and the

PLATE IV

29.

Plate IV shows doll and her clothing.

hat above it is white with pink and white striped crown and streamers and a red bow. The dress at the lower right-hand side is sky blue with dark gray bands to match the dark gray bonnet with blue trimmings and tie.

Plate V, No. 30, shows a doll with cheeks lightly tinted, light tan hair and slippers. The costume consists of a red shawl, light green skirt and white apron.

The baby in Plate VI, No. 31, has the same coloring as the other dolls mentioned. Her clothes are all white with the exception of the ribbons. The

PLATE V

30.

Plate V, doll with lightly tinted cheeks, light hair.

long dress has pale lavender ribbon and toy, and the little costume in the upper right-hand corner has blue ribbons and blue slippers.

In Plate VII, No. 32, the sack is light tan with blue ribbons and bands, with lace ruffles. The bonnet rim is pink and white striped, with a touch of gray directly underneath at each side; the remaining trimming and tie are pink. A white dress directly underneath the sack has a corsage of pink flowers.

The only coloring, aside from the dolls, in Plate VIII, No. 33, is light tan for the dress at lower right, white shawl and ruffles at sleeves. Shoes and slippers are light tan except for the tiniest doll, which has white shoes.

PLATE VI

31.

Plate VI, baby doll dressed all in white except ribbons.

Plate VII, doll has light tan sack with blue ribbons and bands, with lace ruffles.

PLATE VIII

33.

Plate VIII, dress at right is light tan.

The little girl in Plate IX (No. 34) is the proud possessor of three dresses and one hat. The upper right is white with pink stripes and the apron is pale green, the dress in the lower left is blue; apron and cat, tannish pink. The costume in the lower right-hand side is magenta red with a white apron and pink shoes. A tan basket contains pink and blue flowers similar to that of the decoration on the dress.

The lone little boy in Plate X (35) wears a pink blouse with white collar and cuff and light tan pants. His newsboy costume consists of a light blue

Plate IX, doll has three dresses and hat.

coat, black pants, and tan hat; schoolboy costume, light blue pants, black jacket and shoes, white collar and cuffs, and a tan hat with red band. The dress-up costume in the lower right of plate consists of a white blouse with blue tie, tan trousers and belt, black shoes, red jacket trimmed with black to match the hat. The band of the latter matches the pants.

PLATE X

35

Plate X, schoolboy and his clothes.

The title page and text of the booklet reads as follows:

"Paper Dolls, and How to Make Them—a—Book for Little Girls. New Edition, Improved and Enlarged—New York: Anson D. F. Randolph, 683 Broadway, 1857—Entered according to Act of Congress, in the year 1856, by Anson D. F. Randolph, in the Clerk's Office of the District Court for the Southern District of New York—John A. Gray's Fireproof Printing Office. 16 and 18 Jacob Street, N. Y.

"My Dear Young Friends:

"I have often pitied myself, because there were no Paper Dolls when I was a little girl. I supposed that all little girls, now-a-days, played with them, until a few days ago, when a lady told me that she knew a number, who had never heard of Paper Dolls, and then she said: 'Why can't you make a little book, and tell how to make them?' and Mary looked up and said: 'Please, do, Mamma, it would make a great many children happy.' So, as I am kept in my room, not able to do much else, I will try to teach you how to enjoy this delightful amusement.

"All that I knew about Paper Dolls when I was a little girl was, that sometimes a kind friend would cut from a long, narrow strip of paper, (usually the edge of a newspaper,) folded a great many times, so that all could be cut at once, a row of little men and women, like this:

or this:

Even these poor little things were very amusing.

"Eight or nine years ago, I first saw a genuine modern Paper Doll. It was cut out of Bristol board, and painted to represent a little girl, very fat, with a very small waist, and a very high forehead, and red cheeks, and a great quantity of curls. It had three dresses, one pink, one blue, and one yellow, of different fashions, and a hat trimmed with flowers and ribbons. The dresses and the hat were also made of paper, painted very nicely, and could be taken off and put on again. My little girl had never before had any toy, which gave her so much delight. This was the beginning, in our family, of the reign of Paper Dolls, which has lasted, without interruption, to the present day.

"There are now a great many Paper Dolls in the country. I have seen many, made by the same person, who made the one that I have described. She is a little girl in Boston, who, I have heard, is paying for her education, by the money which she receives from the sale of them. They have been sold, for many years, at the book-store of Monroe & Francis, in Boston, where, I presume, they are still to be found. From different parts of New-England, and even from New-York, little girls have sent to this store for a 'lady,' or a 'girl,' or a 'boy,' or a 'family,' and have been delighted at receiving, in exchange for their shilling, or quarter or half-dollar, an envelope, containing the doll and its pretty wardrobe, larger or smaller, with more or fewer dresses, according to its price.

"Then, of late years, there have been 'Jenny Linds,' and other famous ladies, with their elegant wardrobes. 'Fanny Gray,' too, with her history, and dresses to match, is a beautiful toy. These are engraved and richly colored, and made to stand upon a wooden pedestal, by fitting into a groove. They are intended to be admired and respected, but are quite too stately to be treated with familiarity. They can not be taken to the heart, and petted, like our Paper Dolls. Yet for those who do not enjoy the simpler and more varied pleasure of making them for themselves, these are very delightful.

"There is also a less expensive kind of ready-made dolls, printed, and sometimes colored, a dozen or more upon the same sheet of paper, with a dress and hat to fit each one, upon another sheet. The dolls and dresses have only to be cut out, and put together, and then they can go a-visiting, or do any thing which other dolls can do. But they are not what I mean by Paper Dolls.

"What I mean by Paper Dolls are little home-made figures of boys, girls, ladies, babies, any bodies, drawn on paper. and cut out, and dressed in paper clothes. These dolls and dresses may be pencilled or painted, they may be well made or badly made, they may look like elegant ladies, and dear little babies, or they can be cross-eyed, and their foreheads may be larger than all the rest of their faces, and their heads may grow out of their shoulders, and their fat arms may stand out straight, and end in little knobs, it is all the same, they are 'little darlings,' 'perfect beauties,' 'the sweetest little things that ever were seen,' and nothing in the way of paper is too good to cut up and make their dresses.

"And this is one of the charms of Paper-Doll-playing. Out of an old card, and a few bits of colored paper, with the aid of a pencil and a pair of scissors, a child can create for herself a world of enjoyment. Babies to be nursed and fondled, little girls and boys to be taught and entertained, rewarded and punished, mammas to keep house and go visiting, and take care of the little ones, with an endless variety of dresses suited to all occasions, are fashioned by their little fingers, with as much delight as they receive from the most expensive doll, which has come all the way from London or Paris. I have often been surprised at the ingenuity and taste which children have shown, in designing the different articles of dress, out of almost nothing. Little bits of paper which would else have been thrown away as useless, acquire a new value. 'What a beautiful basque this will make for my "little Lilly!"' 'Here's a piece of gold paper;' perhaps it is half an inch long by an eighth of an inch wide; 'it will make some buttons and a buckle for "little Freddy's" jacket.' Even the stray feather escaped from a pillow, a nuisance to all other eyes, is seized upon as a treasure, and converted into a graceful ornament, as all must allow, to 'little Willy's' cap.

"But I suppose that you want to see one of these wonderful Paper Dolls, if you are so unfortunate as never to have had that pleasure. So I must make haste and tell you how to make them.

"What are they made of?

"Any kind of stiff paper, the backs of old cards, pasteboard, Bristol boards; the finer and smoother and cleaner it is, so much the better. A glazed, 'shiny' surface will not answer, for you can not draw the face well upon it.

"For the dresses, I dare say that your father will give you the colored covers of old pamphlets. The unprinted backs of these are better than the glazed colored papers which you find at the book-stores, because you can paint upon them, and thus shade and trim them as you please. The folds are made by painting with a darker shade of the same color. Some of the prettiest dresses which I have seen, have been made of white paper, painted, but it requires more labor and skill to make them well in this way, than of paper already colored. There is scarcely any kind of paper, even brown wrapping-paper, ont of which you can not make something pretty for your little ladies and gentlemen. Colored note-paper or letter-paper is perhaps the most desirable material. The colored tissue 'motto-papers' make elegant dresses for parties, if you allow your little people to go to such places. Of plain white paper you can, with the help of a pencil, make beautiful embroidered jackets, and aprons and baby dresses.

"These are the materials. Now we are ready to begin.

"You will need a 'pattern,' to guide you in your first attempts. You will find several at the end of the book. Take a piece of thin paper, and lay it over one of these, and trace it. Cut out the figure that you have drawn, and you will thus have a pattern, which you can lay upon stiff paper, and draw its outline by passing your pencil around its edge. Cut out this stiff one for your first Paper Doll, and I wish you much joy in playing with it.

"Next draw the hair and features as well as you can. Try to make the eyebrows alike, and the eyes of the same size, and looking the same way, and the nose in the middle, and do not let the mouth stretch quite from one ear to the other. The curls, I dare say, will have rather a singular appearance; but never mind, you'll do better by and by. It would be well to practice making faces upon your slate. I presume that almost every child has some older friend, who will be very glad to assist her in both drawing and painting the faces of her dolls.

"If, after your first doll is finished, you should say, 'What a horrid-looking thing!' which I do not believe you will say, do not destroy it, but make a dress for it, and give it to your little sister, and she, I am sure, will be delighted, and call it 'pooty baby.' Then try again, and make another, and if this second one does not look as well as you hoped it would, still I think that you had best make a dress or two for it; for after all, the great charm of 'playing Paper Dolls' is in dressing them. If you can not succeed in making respectable-looking faces, you can perhaps find in some 'fashion-plate' at the end of an old magazine, a suitable head, which your mother will allow you to cut off, and paste upon a body of your own making, for these fashionable things have no real bodies; their dress is the whole of them.

"For such, and many other purposes, you will find a bottle of gum Arabic very useful. Two or three pennies' worth of gum, dissolved in water, will last you a long time. There are bottles which come on purpose, with wide mouths, and a camel's hair brush fastened into the cork. With a bottle of gum Arabic, you are prepared to do great things in the millinery and dress-making line.

"In order to help you a little, I will draw some Dolls for you. On Plate I. are a boy and girl. You have only to cut them out, and they are ready to be dressed. As I said before, playing with Paper Dolls consists more in dressing them than in making them. It is the dressing them which makes all the difference between paper pictures and Paper Dolls. Even those, who can make them for themselves, are much pleased to have new patterns made for them. So I will proceed at once to the dressing, for I am in a great hurry to have you begin.

"Now the great invention, from which Paper-Doll playing may be said to have its beginning, consists simply in making the dresses doubled at the top, so that they may stay on. I consider this one of the greatest discoveries of modern times. As soon as paper frocks could be kept on paper shoulders, you may be sure that there were plenty of little fingers ready to put them on. The way is simply this; to *fold the paper* of which the dress is to be made, having the fold at the top, so that the dress is cut double, front and back, and the folded part makes a shoulder-strap. You will understand this by looking at the print. (Plate III. Fig. 2.)

"In order to make the dress fit the doll, you must lay the doll upon the folded paper, and mark the paper so that it will fit at the neck and the belt, and, as far as possible, draw the outline of the sleeves, waist and skirt, according to your fancy. Then remove the doll, and finish the outline and cut it out. Plate III Figs. 1 and 2, will make this plain.

"Be careful and do not cut the shoulder-straps so narrow, that they will be torn open the first time that the dress is put on. And yet the space must not be too wide, or it will look very awkwardly. If your paper is scant, it is not necessary that the back should be the whole length of the front, for only the front is painted and ornamented and expected to be looked at.

"Now that you have learned this great secret, the way is clear before you. You can make dresses to your hearts' content, long waists, short waists, long skirts, short skirts, long sleeves, short sleeves, flounces and furbelows.

"You have as yet learned to make only low-necked dresses, which can be slipped on over the head. But certainly the little ladies will need some high-necked dresses for winter. I am sure that you would not send your doll to school with nothing on her neck. Yet you can not expect her head, if it is paper, to go through a hole, which is only big enough for her neck. So what can you do?

"Make the neck of the dress to fit the doll's throat, and then cut a slit down the back; or, what is still better cut the back like Fig. 2. Plate IV.

"Jackets, aprons, cloaks, mantillas are all fastened in the same way. Collars and belts can be neatly fitted, by making them long enough to fold over on the back, as represented in Plate II. Figs. 1 and 2.

"Bonnets and caps are made of two parts, the back and front, cut in the same shape, and gummed at the edges, leaving barely room for the head to slip in.

"It is a good plan to keep each doll, with its wardrobe, in an envelope by itself. My little girls name their dolls, and write their names and ages upon their backs, and upon the backs of their clothes. You will see how useful this would be, in case one of the little ones, who can not talk, should get lost.

"I have given you directions for only the simplest and easiest way of making dresses. You will learn to vary from them in some respects. In Plate V you will see that the cloak can not be doubled at the top. The edges of the front and back are gummed together at the *sides*, leaving a space large enough for the head and shoulders to slip through.

"In Plate VIII. Fig. 2, the white neck-kerchief which is gummed to the dress, is folded behind, leaving an opening for the head.

"In cases where one or both arms fall within the dress, like Plate III. Fig. 1, you can either cut out the lower part of the arm, so that the dress will fit beneath it, or draw and paint a false arm, as in the baby's dress (Plate VI.) or cut one from card-board, and gum it to the sleeve.

"In the sack Fig. 3, Plate III., cut a slit at the bottom of the sleeve, and slip the arm through it.

"Collars, cuffs, belts, buttons, trimmings, under-sleeves, pantalettes, even legs with shoes and stockings, can be cut out and gummed to the dresses, or, when the dress is painted upon white paper, the white articles can be left unpainted, and shaded and ornamented at pleasure.

"I think that you now know enough to be left to yourselves. You will find patterns of various articles of dress for boys, and girls, and ladies, and babies, at the end of the book. These are not to be cut out, but to be copied. There is no end to the pretty things that you can make. You will soon collect, in one way or another, the simple materials which you can convert into beautiful dresses. I am sure that you and your mothers will all agree with me in saying that playing with Paper Dolls is the most delightful, the most varied, and at the same time the most simple and the least expensive of all your amusements."

Chapter V

The Jenny Lind Paper Doll

THE Jenny Lind paper doll! To collectors the name is magic, for few are fortunate enough to possess such a coveted item. We wonder how many of the original dolls escaped the trash barrel when the small owners of long ago outgrew childish pursuits and did not have the sentiment or foresight to keep so fine a souvenir of one of the greatest singers and actresses of the nineteenth century. There were many souvenirs of the "Swedish Nightingale," and many persons have spent a lifetime collecting them. Her picture appeared on boxes, bottles, handkerchiefs, etc., and articles of clothing as well as babies and pets were named after her. From a broadside printed by F. Hodges in London, when the lady captivated all England with her remarkable talents, we get an inkling of this:

"Now everything is Jenny Lind,
    That comes out new each day,
"There's Jenny Lind Shawls and bonnet too,
    For those who cash can pay,
"Jenny Lind's coats and waistcoats,
    Shirts, whiskers too and stocks,
"Jenny Lind's gowns and petticoats,
    And bustles such a lot.

"If to a butcher's shop you go,
    To buy a joint of meat,
"It's buy, oh buy, my Jenny Lind,
    She's tender and she's sweet,
"And the greasy little butcher's boys,
    Sing with a knowing grin,
"Eightpence a pound this splendid leg,
    Is fit for Jenny Lind.

"For gents smoke nought but Jenny Lind,
    For so they name Cigars,
"And shop boys for to come out slap
    Smoke Jenny Lind by halves.
"And ladies who a shopping go,
    To the Mercer's will drop in,
"And ask for a yard and a half of silk
    Cut off of Jenny Lind."

There were many more verses equally poor, but all giving homage to the famous Jenny Lind.

To the doll collector the best souvenir of the singer is, of course, a real Jenny Lind doll or a paper doll of the lady. The *Museum of the City of New York* has both. The *Essex Museum* in Salem, Mass., and the *Newark, N. J. Museum* have well preserved specimens of the paper doll and her outfits, and there probably are other museums in this country and abroad which are equally fortunate.

Most of us think of Jenny Lind only as a singer, but she was much more than that. Her acting ability was superb, and to the end of her sixty-seven years, in 1887, she was completely unspoiled by fame or the perils which beset the stage of her time. She made friends with the great, and listened with sympathetic ear to the troubles of the most humble. Her kindness and generosity in big ways and little knew no bounds.

An interesting incident occurred while she was in Boston on a concert tour. The attention of Jenny Lind was called to a young servant girl who had spent a half month's wages on a ticket to a Lind concert. During the course of the evening the servant girl received a note from the singer in which was enclosed a twenty-dollar gold piece.

On another occasion, this time in England, when she sought release from pressure in a lone walk through the countryside, she became tired and asked a cottager if she might rest with her and her children for a little while. In the course of the conversation, in which, by the way, it was disclosed that her husband had been ill and out of work, and consequently had suffered financial lack, the mistress of the house asked if she had heard the famous singer Jenny Lind.

"Yes," answered Jenny, "I have heard her many times."

"How I wish I might have that pleasure," was the comment.

"If you like, I will sing for you," said Jenny, suiting the action to the words. The housewife was enchanted; never had she heard such a voice.

"Now," said Jenny, "you may tell your friends that you have heard Jenny Lind." Then, with a grateful farewell, Jenny pressed into the hand she shook what at first seemed to the woman of the house a crumpled piece of paper. It was a bank note for five pounds. But before the recipient realized what had happened Jenny was out of sight.

The early life of Jenny Lind was not without trouble, financially and in other ways. Her mother, although well educated, was harsh and unyielding and resentful that Herr Lind could not make enough money to support the family without her help. She took out her irritation on the child. But Jenny had a respite when she went to live with her beloved grandmother at the Widows' House. It was while living here that a dancer at the Royal Opera House, Mademoiselle Lundberg, chanced to hear Jenny sing to her cat, was delighted with the child's voice, and used her influence to have the nine-year-old girl accepted for the Royal Theatre School at the expense of the government. Count Puke, head of the theatre, at first looked upon Jenny with disdain, saying that such an ugly little thing never could become an actress or a dancer. When he heard the child sing, his attitude changed quickly. She proved her worth far beyond his wildest dreams in the years that followed.

Jenny's girlhood years as an "actress pupil" did not give her much opportunity to use her voice, for hers were mainly speaking parts at that time. Later, at about twenty, when touring the provinces in Sweden giving concerts in order to raise money for special voice training in Paris under the noted teacher García, she used her voice too much. It became so strained that she almost defeated her purpose, for García at first refused to accept her as a pupil. Finally he told her to take a rest of three weeks, not to sing a note during that time and talk as little as possible, then come to him again for a try-out. The second try-out resulted in nearly a year's training under this expert teacher. and her voice not only was completely restored, but immeasurably enriched. Before leaving Stockholm for Paris Jenny had enchanted her native people by singing as Norma in the opera by the same name as a farewell gesture. Upon returning from Paris she played the same role, and the audience were amazed and delighted with her progress. And when she took the part of Amine in "La Somnambule" they declared her voice unrivalled by any other singer.

Much has been said of Jenny Lind's plainness, and how she was transformed when acting and singing. Once at a musical party given for the Princess of Prussia, Lady Westmorland remarked, on seeing the singer for the first time, "Why—she is not only pale, thin and plain-featured, but awkward and rather nervous. Exactly like a country schoolgirl! It is preposterous." When questioned afterward about the performance, Lady Westmorland enthusiastically exclaimed, "She is simply an angel . . . . when she began to sing her face shone like an angel. I never saw or heard anything in the least like it." The box cover of the Jenny Lind paper doll (No. 36) was copied, partly from memory, from one in the *Museum of the City of New York*.

Jenny Lind, the paper doll, (No. 37, Figure 1), is pictured as a blonde, the natural coloring of the actress, although most of her real doll representatives are brunettes. It has been said that she preferred dark hair. However this might be, one rarely finds a blonde Jenny Lind doll, perhaps for the reason that most china-headed dolls have black hair; black shows to greater advantage against the white china face and shoulders. Notice how the hair is slicked to the side of the head. This is to allow room for the separate wig to be attached. Notice also the flat-soled slippers. This was a period when high heels had not yet been re-introduced in Europe.

Figure No. 2 is the costume Jenny wore in her first great success—as Agatha in Carl Maria von Weber's *Der Freischütz,* or *The Seventh Bullet.* The words are by Friedrich Kind. It was first produced in Berlin a year after the birth of Jenny Lind. The story centers around Agathe, engaged to Max, the man who has been named successor to the ageing Kuno, head ranger, and father of Agathe. In order to accept the position, Max has to prove himself a skilled marksman in a hunting match. The villain of the play is Casper, who has sold himself to the devil, Zamiel. Through Casper's black magic, Max is caused to miss the mark so many times that he is completely discouraged in the rehearsals for the match. Then Casper promises that if Max will meet him at the Wolf's Glen, all will be well, for he will be given magic bullets. In the meantime Agathe has been warned of what is afoot by a hermit of the woods and presented with a magic wreath of roses to counteract the evil. When the day of the match comes, six of the charmed bullets hit the mark, but the prince orders the seventh to be aimed at a dove, which is really Agathe in disguise. Agathe falls wounded to the ground, but the magic wreath does its work and she lives to wear it on her wedding day.

Although Jenny was used to a responsive audience, this was to be until now her longest and most important role. The girl was so frightened beforehand that she could not touch food or drink, but when the time came her fear vanished, and she lived the part of the Bohemian peasant girl Agathe with such feeling that the audience went wild with enthusiasm. Even the orchestra laid down its instruments to applaud the eighteen-year-old girl. In remembrance of this

Box cover from the Jenny Lind Paper Doll.

occasion the directors of the Royal Theatre sent her a gorgeous pair of silver candlesticks, to her utter delight.

Agathe's costume consists of a yellow skirt and blue bodice, the latter trimmed in lighter blue. A white blouse shows at the neck. The ribbon sash is pink.

No. 3 represents the costume of Mary or Marie in Gaetano Donizetti's (words by Bayard St. Georges) *The Daughter of the Regiment,* first produced

2. "The Freischütz" as Agathe

3. "The Daughter of the Regiment" as Mary

Fig. 37.
Jenny Lind

Costumes for two of Jenny Lind's roles.

in France in 1840, with Anna Thillon as Vivandiere. Seven years later it was given in London as an Italian opera, with Jenny Lind in the role of Mary.

The scene is laid in the Tyrol during its occupation by the French. Mary, the adopted daughter of the 21st Regiment under Napoleon, was found on the field after a battle by Sulpice, one of the soldiers. The opera opens with Mary as a young woman singing *The Camp was my Birthplace,* followed by a duet with Sulpice, *The Rataplan,* a rousing martial air accompanied by drums and brasses. The Regiment is celebrating. A Tyrolean peasant, Tony, has just rescued Mary, with whom he is in love, from falling over a precipice. Now, after Tony is cleared of a spy charge, the Regiment has consented to the marriage if Tony will join the Regiment. When everything is set for the marriage the Marchioness of Berkenfeld comes forward and claims Mary as her niece, proving relationship by a letter which was pinned to the child's clothing when she was found. This letter was written to the Marchioness by the father of the girl. The Marchioness takes Mary to live in her castle with the admonition to forget all about Tony. Then the Marchioness reveals that she is really Mary's mother, not her aunt as at first claimed, that in early life she had secretly been married to a man of lower social status than her own. She insists that Mary must not make the same mistake by marrying Tony. However, after a lapse of time, when Tony comes again seeking the hand of his lady-love, this time as Colonel of his Regiment, the Marchioness relents, remembering at last her own feelings when she was a girl in love, and the two are married amid great rejoicing.

The role was especially suited to Jenny. As a child of four she had astonished her folks by picking up and playing by ear on the piano military songs she had heard on the street. Delight in martial music, the sound of drums and rollicking songs stayed with her throughout life, a joy she easily communicated to her audience. Americans loved Jenny in this opera, and today one occasionally finds sheet music of one of the arias from *The Daughter of the Regiment* with the picture of Jenny Lind on the cover. One such, found in a Boston second-hand book shop, is reproduced here.* It would make an excellent paper doll.

In her part as Mary, Jenny wore on her first entrance a black bodice highlighted with bright embroidery, a wide striped skirt in light blue, and a perky bonnet with a white cockade. In her light hair, worn in rolls on either side of the head, was a red rose. The paper doll costume probably was taken from the second of Mary's costumes in the opera. It consists of a light blue bodice with red collar and cuffs, and red edging on the bandoleer or belt worn over the shoulder. To the latter is attached a yellow keg. The skirt is deep blue with a gold band edged with red running diagonally down the front. The dots indicated in the sketch are gold in color. Shoes and belt are black.

No. 4, the costume for Anna in Mozart's *Il Don Giovanni,* or *Don Juan,* consists of a long black cloak edged with yellow and black lace, a typical Spanish costume. The dress showing underneath is light blue to match the ostrich feathers in the headpiece. The wig is black, decorated with a red rose. The black laced boots are high and pointed.

Don Juan, the villain in the opera, falls in love with Donna Anna, who is engaged to another. The rascal tries to steal her at night, but Anna's cries awaken her father. In the ensuing struggle, the father is killed, and Giovanni

*See the frontispiece.

lives to perpetrate more devilish crimes, including murder. In the end, Giovanni himself is destroyed by a statue erected to the memory of one of his victims. The statue comes to life and warns the evil-doer that unless he repents he soon will die. Giovanni laughs and invites the statue to a feast at his house the following day. While the guests are assembled at the banquet table, a knock is heard and the statue enters, and clutching Giovanni in its cold marble hands, again urges repentance. Giovanni refuses, whereupon the statue disappears, demons arise in its place and carry Giovanni away to the region of fire and brimstone.

Costumes No. 5 and No. 9 indicate on the inside lid of the paper doll box that the name of the opera, as well as its principal character, is *Vielka*. Giacomo Meyerbeer at first called his opera *Das Feldlager in Schlesien (A Camp in Silesia)* but after many successes with "the Lind" as Vielka, he re-named it simply *Vielka*. Costume No. 5 consists of a light blue over-dress embroidered and piped with yellow, yellow band on sleeve, which is also lined with the same color, and a yellow skirt trimmed with large dark blue tabs, edged with lighter blue. The wig is yellow, the boots red.

The role of *Vielka*, the Silesian peasant girl, was eminently suited to Jenny's out-door-loving nature, and she played it superbly. A German newspaper said of her acting that both her dramatic and imitative expression were richly employed in the scene in which, by the exercise of her magic art, she "terrifies, tames, charms, cajoles the wild country-folk—One could not only foresee that the wild warriors would follow her, but could feel that they had no choice but to do so."

No. 6, Norma, consists of a white dress and blue cape. The disk and sickle in hand are yellow, matching the hair. A green wreath encircles the head.

The part of Norma in the opera by Vincenzo Bellini introduced Jenny Lind to the German public. She was the unhappy Druid high priestess who, in defiance of her faith, has secretly married Pollione, the Roman proconsul, only to find him unfaithful to her. In her fury she plans vengeance, but when Pollione is brought before her, love is the stronger force in her nature. She tears the secret wreath from her head and declares herself the sinner. Pollione learns the true worth of Norma too late. Both perish together on the funeral pyre. The opera is full of beautiful and inspiring music, including the exquisite prayer *Casta Diva*, still in popular favor. Jenny's interpretation of Norma was greeted with thunderous applause, and her success in Germany was assured. She was appointed "Imperial Royal Chamber Singer."

No. 7, Valentine's costume in *The Huguenots*, is red with yellow insets in the skirts of some of the doll sets. In others the insets are white-edged with blue ruffles and blue bows between, the bows decorated with yellow buckles. Collar and sleeve linings are white in some sets, blue in others, and the girdle yellow. A wig of black corkscrew curls comes with this outfit.

The Huguenots, by Giacomo Meyerbeer, is a dramatic opera telling of the love of Valentine St. Bris for a nobleman, Raoul de Nangis. The latter, thinking Valentine is pledged to another, Count de Nevers, renounces his hopes. As a matter of fact, she had been pledged to Count de Nevers, but had called it off because she really was in love with Raoul. Valentine, urged to marry Count de Nevers, goes to a chapel to pray, and from within the chapel hears of a plot

4. "Don Juan" as
Donna Anna

5. "Vielka" as Vielka

6. "Norma" as Norma

"The Huguenots" as
Valentine

Jenny Lind's costumes in the roles indicated.

to assassinate Raoul. She communicates this news to Marcel, Raoul's faithful Huguenot servant, and the latter organizes a party of Huguenots to rescue his master. Then a plot is conceived by Catherine de Médici for the slaughter of the Huguenots, and Raoul, concealed by Valentine behind the tapestries, over-hears what is going on. He warns the Huguenots of their danger and goes back to the chapel, where many of the Huguenots have taken refuge. Here Valentine joins him, and with the blessing of Marcel, who, though wounded, has come to tell his master of the death of De Nevers, the two are united, and all perish together in the massacre.

No. 8, the costume for Amine in *The Somnambule, The Sleep Walker*, con-sists of a yellow skirt with red bands at the bottom and a blue bodice trimmed with yellow over a white blouse, contrasting with the red lining of the cape, which shows at the back and the red tie at neckline. The yellow cap has red streamers, and a pink rose adorns the yellow hair.

Jenny, as Amine, so thoroughly lived her part that the audience was tense as she sang of her unjust accusations while she walked in her sleep over the treacherous mill-stream bridge, which gave way under her feet as she sang. She might have had a substitute take the risks involved, but refused, saying she would be ashamed to face her audience pretending she had crossed the bridge. Hans Christian Andersen said of Jenny in her role as Amine, "Nobody could see her in *La Somnambule* and not go away a better man. She is not so great a singer as Malibran, but a better actress—and the most amiable child I have ever known. In private life she seemed to me an ennobled Cinderella."

No. 9 is another costume for *Vielka*. It has a brightly embroidered red bodice with gold trimmings, and a brownish purple skirt with red bands, the latter edged with gold tassels. The cap is red with gold trimming. The pointed red shoes have colored lacings.

No. 10, the costume for Alice in *Robert the Devil*, Meyerbeer's opera, con-sists of a brown coat with blue sash, collar and tie, and squares on the cape. The hat is black with a touch of blue.

Jenny, as Alice, played the part of the good foster sister of Robert, son of the Devil by marriage to a human woman. Robert is being led into temptation constantly by his notorious father, the Devil, disguised as a friend, Bertram. Finally, through the untiring efforts of Alice, the spell is broken and Robert is free to marry the girl of his choice, Isabella of Sicily.

This was the first of the operas in England in which Jenny Lind starred, a long-looked-for event and much publicized. Queen Victoria, who had al-ready made Jenny's acquaintance in Europe, and was a devotee, was in the intense, eager, excited audience. The opera was an immense success, and when the curtains fell, Jenny made her call before a wildly applauding audience. The young queen—she was about the same age as Jenny—threw a magnificent bouquet of flowers at the feet of the singer.

No. 11 is Jenny Lind's concert costume. It is colored differently, but is the same dress as that shown on the figure decorating the box-cover. The over-dress is light pink with a light lace collar and cuff bands, the skirt light blue. There are matching blue feathers in the headgear and a gold crown. A red rose decorates the hair. On the box cover the overdress is red with a white collar, and the skirt is yellow.

"The Somnambule"
as Amine

"Vielka" as Vielka

"Robert the Devil"
as Alice

In the Concert Toilette

Jenny Lind's costumes in the roles named.

Chapter VI

Paper Doll Dancers of the Romantic Ballet

THE great romantic ballet dancers of the first half of the nineteenth century brought forth their quota of paper doll representatives. Whether or not all of these famous dancers delighted children with their paper images is not known to the writer, but two of them, Marie Taglioni and Fanny Elssler, were so honored, and it is more than likely that such popular dancers as Carlotta Grisi and Fanny Cerrito appeared in paper doll form. It is for this reason that the two last named dancers are illustrated here.

Herbert H. Hosmer, Jr., of South Lancaster, Massachusetts, says in his article *Paper Dancers* in the December 1948 number of *Antiques:*

"During the 1840 period, when ballerinas were the toast of two continents, manufacturers of paper dolls abroad brought out boxes of these dancers with costumes illustrating the dances associated with them. These probably came in various sizes, for Fanny Elssler is less than five inches tall while Marie Taglioni is nine inches tall. The latter is identified on the cover as Taglioni, First Dancer of Paris. She has five headdresses and six costumes with arms arranged in dance positions. Marie herself is posed on her toes. The costumes have backs as well as fronts and are hand-tinted and glazed. Fanny Elssler's pink, green and gilt box has a tinted illustration on the cover representing her in The Cachucha, after the familiar print. She is identified only as The Dancer of Paris, but the costume for The Cachucha determines her identity. She has six costumes in typical pose, and three headdresses. These dolls were apparently produced for the English, French and German trade."

Mr. Hosmer also touches on the famous dancing children of the nineteenth century, Augusta Maywood and Mary Ann Lee, who might, he says, have inspired his uncle, John Greene Chandler of Boston, Massachusetts, to publish in 1857 *Little Fairy Lightfoot,* one of a series of paper dolls.

The first great romantic ballet, and one which brought Marie Taglioni to the limelight, was "La Sylphide" produced in 1832, and composed by Marie's father, Philippe Taglioni, for his daughter. This ballet is often confused with a much later production, *Les Sylphides,* by Michel Fokine. Costumes for the latter are illustrated in a modern *Ballet Dancing Coloring Book,* by Merrill Co. of Chicago, Illinois, and *Les Sylphides* is described as one of the most beautiful and famous of all ballets. It was for the earlier *La Sylphide* that Eugène Lami created the classic full white skirt reaching half way to the ankle which then became standard. It was used by Carlotta Grisi in *Giselle,* 1841 (revived in 1940); in *Les Sylphides* about the turn of the century, and to this day is the standard ballet costume. Once in a while one comes across an old handpainted copy of a ballet dancer which might represent one of these celebrities. The four illustrated were very popular.

Taglioni (No. 38) was born in Stockholm in 1804. She was considered by many to be the greatest of all the romantic female dancers, an opinion well earned. Hers was the case of the ugly duckling growing up to become a swan. Mocked and derided, for her ill-formed little body, by her childhood companions at dancing school, she grew up to be the rival of them all. But she was born to dance; she came of a dancing family. Her father and grandfather were famous dancers. Dancing transformed her plainness into fairy-like beauty; she was phenomenal.

There are few paintings of Taglioni. A. E. Chalon gives a side view in the beautiful painting, 1845 of the *Three Graces,* including Fanny Elssler and Fanny Cerrito. Taglioni's dancing had an ethereal quality; she seemed to float through the air and descend gradually, a quality, she explained, acquired by her method of breathing. Classical ballet, as it is danced today, on the toes or on the "pointes," was started by Marie Taglioni.

Pollock's *Ladies of the Chorus,* printed in London about 1832 to represent *The Silver Palace,* a juvenile drama, pictures costumes similar in style to one worn by Marie Taglioni in *La Sylphide.* The ballet of this period abounded in the supernatural. *La Sylphide* was the story of a wood nymph who fell in love with a mortal. If it had been written at an earlier period, *La Sylphide* might have flown through the air by means of wires from above like a puppet fairy, but thanks to Taglioni, dancing on the toes to suggest aerial movement had by this time superseded the wires.

The robust, dynamic, and magnetic personal charm of the most popular of all the ballet dancers of the 1830's and 1840's, Fanny Elssler, a Viennese, born in 1810, (see No. 40), contrasted strongly to the ethereal but plain-featured Marie Taglioni. Elssler's dances suited her character. They were adaptations of peppy folk dances given with astounding vigor. After conquering Europe she took New York by storm, then Boston, Baltimore, Washington "and all points South." In Boston she made an offer of her ballet slippers to be auctioned off, the proceeds to go toward the completion of Bunker Hill Monument. The slippers disappeared, and some say they are sealed in the cornerstone of the Monument. In New York and again in Baltimore her carriage was unhitched, and Fanny was carried to the opera house in triumph on the shoulders of enthusiastic young men. In Washington this Viennese dancer had the Senate and House in a dither, not to mention the president himself—Martin Van Buren— and his son John. For a while the president was not on speaking terms with John, for the latter had more charm for Fanny than his father. In New Orleans so loud were the serenades, the cheers, and songs underneath the lady's hotel window that finally a fight ensued between the noise makers and those who wished for quiet, and the party had to be broken up by police. All this delighted Fanny. Her stay in America, which was to have lasted for two weeks, extended to two years, and she left the country richer by ninety thousand dollars.

Fanny Elssler's rise to fame surpasses all the fairy tales. She was one of six children in a far from wealthy home. Her father was a valet. He also copied music for the composer Haydn, but his income was not sufficient for so large a family. Mother Elssler helped out by needlework and laundry. Nevertheless, they were able to send Fanny and her sister Theresa to dancing school at a tender age. By the time Fanny was seven she danced the leading role of the ballet *La Fée,* and at fourteen she danced at the Royal Court in Naples. By 1835 she was the toast of Paris, then set out to conquer London and America.

According to Fanny, although as a young girl she had many infatuations, the only real love she ever experienced was for Hans Stuhlmuller, an impecunious

Famous dancers represented in paper dolls: Taglioni, Grisi, Elssler, and Cerrito.

young man but a good dancer. One of her infatuations was with the Duc de Reichstadt, son of Napoleon Bonaparte and Marie Louisa of Austria. The Duc was willing to give up his title, family, and fortune to marry the teen-age girl, but Fanny broke off her engagement to him declaring that her art came before everything else. A child born to her by Hans Stuhlmuller was given to relatives to rear. Soon after Elssler's return to Europe from America she retired, at the age of forty-one. She bought a beautiful home with bird sanctuaries, and announced that hereafter she would be the audience while her birds danced. In 1884 this colorful dancer breathed her last. America still has a few souvenirs of Fanny Elssler in the form of her famous portrait on bottles, shirt studs, and paper dolls, all of which should carefully be preserved for future generations to have and cherish; they are worth their weight in gold.

In 1819, the same year that the great Queen Victoria first saw the light of day, little Carlotta Grisi (see No. 39), the third of the great romantic ballet dancers, was born in a hunting lodge of the Hapsburgs near Mantua, Italy. She grew up slender and ever-youthful with "something of the briar rose in her beauty," as Chorley, the English critic, remarked. She might have been an operatic singer, but turned her attention to the ballet at an early age, and at fourteen toured Italy. In her travels she met Jules Perrot, the greatest male ballet dancer and choreographer of his day, and it was he who composed most of the individual dances for this lovely and talented girl. She also danced with Perrot in some of his dances such as *La Esmeralda,* and *La Polka.* It would be interesting to know if he was included in a box of paper dolls of Grisi. The most famous of her roles was *Giselle,* created especially for her by an admirer, Théophile Gautier.

Two years after the birth of Grisi, Fanny Cerrito (see No. 41), the fourth of the famous ballet dancers of the romantic period, was born in Naples, Italy. She also was a beautiful girl, judging from pictures of her in *La Lituana, Ondine, Alma,* and *La Redowa Polka.* She made her debut in San Carlo, but seems to have been a particular favorite in London, where she appeared in Her Majesty's theatre at the age of twenty. It was Jules Perrot who produced the ballet in which she played one of her most famous roles, *Alma ou la Fille de Feu.*

In the illustration Marie Taglioni is dressed in her white *Sylphide* costume, relieved by flowers on dress and hair; Carlotta Grisi also in white in her famous role as *Giselle;* Fanny Elssler in her Spanish costume as Florinda in *The Devil on Two Sticks;* (this outfit is pink with black lace flounces) and Fanny Cerrito in the blue and tan costume she wore in *La Tituana.* The cap in the latter costume is red trimmed with white.

All of these pictures, and many more in full color with backdrop, are given in a delightful book called *The Romantic Ballet,* published by B. T. Batsford, Ltd. The prints in this little book are contemporary, and there is an introduction and notes on the plates by Sacheverell Sitwell. Anyone interested in collecting old paper ballet dolls would find this book interesting and instructive. By familiarizing oneself with the costumes of the dancers, paper dolls of the same might be identified, as was the case with the Fanny Elssler paper doll before mentioned.

The number of homemade, handpainted ballerinas of the 1830-1840 period that turn up in collections attest their popularity.

Chapter VII

Paper Dolls of Raphael Tuck & Sons Company, Ltd.

T O WRITE about and illustrate fully the Raphael Tuck & Sons Company
paper dolls of the 1890's alone would take up so much space that it would
have to be a volume in itself. This chapter can give only an idea of what the
dolls are like. They range in size from five and one-half inches to thirteen inches,
and are beautifully lithographed in full colors. Mrs. Helen W. Jaques of
Marblehead, Massachusetts, has started a check-up of the Raphael Tuck material, but, she says, "it is limitless and the more one works on it the more items
crop up to identify." The check-up has to be entirely among collectors, as the
German blitz of World War II destroyed all the records at headquarters of the
firm in London.

"Lady Edith, No. 4 of Our Pets Series of Dressing Dolls," ten inches high,
is the earliest "child" Raphael Tuck doll the writer has. (Illustration No. 43).
It came before the patented Tuck dolls, and was designed by Margaret McDonald,
who later signed her first name Marguerite. We wonder if success went to her
head. After Lady Edith's patent was applied for, and she was duly copyrighted
in 1894 she ceased to become No. 4 of "Our Pets," but blossomed out as "Artistic
Series I." The only change in the doll itself was that the head was made separately and pasted, at a proper angle, onto an elongated neck, space being left
under the chin to slip on the separate costume which also came with a neck long
enough to allow this manipulation. The earlier "Edith" had slits in the base of
her curls at the shoulders to accomodate tabs on the shoulders of the dress, and
she was an inch shorter, which made her nine inches tall.

"Lady Edith" and three of her later, as well as three of her earlier dresses
are shown with Illustration No. 43. The costumes differ, as only half from each
set are shown.

Artistic series *I F* is light blue with tiny white rings as a pattern in the
cloth. Cuffs are a deeper blue to match the darker stripes in the waist. Bow and
pompon at the waist are white to match the white ruffle around the neck. The
latter is trimmed with light blue embroidery stitches. Gloves and parasol are
yellow, the parasol decorated with a pink ribbon and pompon. The hat is white
with light blue feathers and ribbons.

Artistic Series *I A* is pale yellow dotted with white. An abundance of pink
roses trims the yellow straw hat and the gown. A pale pink ribbon sash and
fan complete the costume. Fringe and fan are a little darker shade.

Both the pale yellow straw hat and pale gray dress, *I D*, are abundantly
trimmed with yellow and plum colored pansies, the dress being trimmed also
with white ruffles, sash and bag. A yellow tassel and draw-string on the latter,

70

Lady Edith
Artistic Series I

42.

Envelope in which the Lady Edith doll came.

Part of Lady Edith's wardrobe.

and yellow trimming above the ruffle of the skirt, add a touch of color. Underneath the trimming on the waist is a plum colored bodice. Ribbons on the hat are white.

Of the earlier costumes, *4 A* is pale yellow with yellow ochre shading and white dots. Bertha and sleeve ruffles are white. Trimming on dress matches the plum colored pansies at the hemline of the skirt. Sleeve ribbon trimmings and hat ribbon have a dotted edge of red to match the ribbon at the neck-line. The hat is yellow with plum colored feathers and ribbon, and a red rose is tucked under the brim.

Outfit *4 C* is pale blue with a darker blue jacket, the latter trimmed with white buttons, revers and sleeve edges to match the white ribbon in the blue hat.

Costume *4 D* consists of a white dress with an overdress in lavender to match the ribbons in the white hat.

This earlier doll came in the box illustrated later on of the same general kind in an envelope. All these dolls stand by means of a cardboard easel attached to the rear. Both the earlier and later doll and costumes have the trade mark of the firm, the easel, and ''Raphael Tuck & Sons Ltd., London, Paris, Berlin, New York, Montreal,'' printed on the reverse side. To this also is added, in the case of the earlier doll, ''Publishers to their Majesties, the King and Queen,'' the later doll, ''By special appointment, publishers to her Majesty, the Queen.''

Little Boy Blue
45

Envelope containing "The Fairy Tale Series of Dressing Dolls."

No. 45 illustrates the envelope (six by nine and one-half inches) which contains "The Fairy Tale Series of Dressing Dolls," Artistic Series X of the Raphael Tuck dolls. It is printed in blue and gold. Dotted lines indicate folds.

The doll itself (No. 46), Prince Charming of Cinderella fame, is marked X, and the American copyright, February 20th, 1894, is indicated on the reverse side of the figure. He has light brown eyes, abundant yellow hair, and wears a tunic costume of light blue, brown shoes, garter, and belt. The latter is studded with yellow jewels, matching the jewels which edge the tunic.

A separate Prince Charming costume, $X A$, is pink, trimmed with deep plum colored, yellow-edged ribbon, yellow and red belt, beads of yellow, blue and red, and a yellow sword studded with pearls and rubies. His cape is a rich plum color with lining of a lighter shade, and is trimmed around the edges with fine, uneven lines of yellow. Cap matches the cloak, and the crown encircling the rim of the cap is gold with a line of large red oblong jewels alternating with green diamond shaped stones. A single pink ostrich plume towers above the cap. A white blouse shows underneath the tunic, matching the "glass" slipper.

Included are three other story book characters, (1) Dick Whittington, $X B$, with green suit and hat. The collar and belt of the suit are brown, matching the shoes. Accompanying him are his worldly possessions tied in a red bandana attached to a stick, and at his feet a gray and white cat. (2) Jack Horner, $X C$,

**Artistic Series VIII, with Red Riding Hood, Mother Goose, Little
Bo Peep costumes; also dotted Swiss white dress over pale blue,
with gray mitts and neckband. At the lower left above is shown
the central figure in the cover design.**

with plum colored suit; white, yellow-dotted apron; white cuff frills and stockings; yellow hat with plum colored band and flowers and gray slippers.   (3) Little Boy Blue, *X D*, with blue smock, gray hat trimmed with blue; white stockings and gray slippers.   His outfit may be seen in the cover design.

Another in *The Fairy Tale Series of Dressing Dolls* is (No. 47), Artistic Series VIII. All these paper dolls look like little angels, and VIII is no exception to the rule. She has flowing wavy light hair tied up with a yellow band to match the yellow ribbon at waist and sleeves of her dainty white underwear. Her blue eyes are wide and wistful. She wears white socks and dark blue slippers. The central cover design shows VIII as Little Red Riding Hood, and VIII A is the separate costume for this character. There is the traditional red cape. The hood to go with it is shown only in the cover design—see illustration "in small." A blue skirt, white apron and socks and brown slippers complete the ensemble.

Mother Goose, VIII B, is red with panniers of dark gray relieved by a yellow flower design to match the lining of the cape and ribbons holding the goose, as well as the ribbon bow on shoulder. Dark gray ribbons fasten the bodice, and these match the bow at neck; bows down center of skirt front, and bands around the bottom of the skirt. Panniers are finished at the waist-line with red ribbon and rosette. Slippers are blue with red heels and bow; red stockings. The goose is white.

Little Bo Peep, VIII D, is a study in lavender and white. The apron and all the ruffles are white, sleeves and panniers white with a lavender design. Bodice, skirt and ribbon ruching and bows are lavender, except for white bows on the shoes. The slippers are a darker shade to match the narrow band around bottom of skirt. The hat is yellow straw with lavender ribbons and white daisies.

No. VIII C is a dainty white dotted Swiss over pale blue. Mitt and neckband are gray, and the bowl is blue on the outside, white within.

The cover design of Artistic Series VIII is the same as the cover design for Series X except for the central figure and the coloring. The former is blue, the latter red.

"Lordly Lionel," Artistic Series V, from *The Prince and Princess Series of Dressing Dolls,* is a blue-eyed blond. He is dressed all in white except for a blue sash and slippers, the latter rimmed with yellow jewels. In the design on the envelope (No. 48), the costume is practically the same as *V C*, except for the coloring, which is in pink and gold on a white background.

The beautiful costume *V A* is light blue with darker blue buttons, tunic and ruffles at sleeves white lace, and the bouquet is of yellow roses. Cap to match is light blue, ruffle, feathers and buckle, white.

V C is in lavender and white, both hat and costume. The darker lines represent a darker shade of lavender.

In the illustrations V B, the parts shaded are light brown, the unshaded parts foliage green.

Lordly Lionel's falconry costume, *V D*, is the most elaborate of all. The blouse is white, the body of the jacket is dark green, edged with yellow, trousers and oversleeves are light green with yellow trimming. Gloves, boots, sash, and hat are greenish gray, the hat trimmed with light blue feather and ribbon, the

LORDLY LIONEL

THE PRINCE AND PRINCESS SERIES OF DRESSING DOLLS

PAT.ᵈ FEB. 20ᵀᴴ 1894.

RAPHAEL TUCK & SONS
LONDON : PARIS : NEW YORK
PUBLISHERS TO HER MAJESTY THE QUEEN

DESIGNED BY MARGUERITE McDONALD

48

Envelope for the Lordly Lionel doll.

Lordly Lionel and his formal costume. Lionel has blue eyes and light hair.

Lordly Lionel's semi-formal outfit (VC); his every-day costume (VB); and his most elaborate one, the hunting costume (VD).

boots and gloves edged with white. Yellow and red embroidery stitches on the gloves gives an added touch of color. The lining of the cape is yellow with yellow ribbon bow on shoulder and around the falcon's leg. The bird is grayish brown with a yellow head, ruff and crown. There is a yellow chain around the neck and yellow buckles on the boots. Tabs are pasted on the shoulder below the standing collar.

"Sweet Abigail," (No. 50), Artistic Series VI of *The Prince and Princess Series of Dressing Dolls,* appears on the cover in the dress VI D. Otherwise, the cover of the envelope is exactly the same as that of the Prince, "Lordly Lionel." Her long, wavy blonde hair shows to advantage with every costume, for, as explained before with all these Artistic Series, the separate head is pasted on an elongated neck leaving plenty of space at the sides for the hair to fall over the shoulders. "Abigail" has blue eyes, a white dotted Swiss dress, pink stockings and slippers, the latter with white bows, and she wears a green band trimmed with pearls in her hair and green ribbon around her waist. Gold bracelets are inset with white pearls.

No. VI A also is a white dress, but elaborately trimmed with deep orange ribbon and orange polka dots in the panniers. Feathers and trimming on the white hat are a shade deeper than the dress trimmings.

Princess Abigail's state robe consists of a white outer dress with fleur de lis figures and dots in lavender, lace around the bottom of the puffed sleeve and neck-line, a yellow skirt trimmed with yellow, green and red jewels, yellow

Sweet Abigail and her costumes for every day (VIA), and for state occasions (VIB).

Sweet Abigail's costumes for the garden (VIC), and for afternoon wear (VID).

slippers and fan, and a yellow mantle lined with lavender. A red and green chain of beads is suspended around her waist, and necklaces are three strands of pearls and a larger strand of alternate large green beads and small yellow ones. The crown is of gold with red, green and yellow jewels and white ostrich feathers.

Costume VI C is a beautiful shade of pink with trimming around the bottom of skirt, slippers and ribbon a deeper pink. There is a white collar and ruching around the upper part of the dress and a white blouse showing underneath. Green and pale yellow beads rim the revers and slashes in sleeves. Pink and yellow roses make a dainty bouquet. Bead trimming on the bag is blue and the crown is yellow with green beads. On the waist is a gold colored crown outlined with red beads, green in center. Necklace consists of red beads or jewels on gold medallion with green jewel pendants.

No. VI D is a lovely shade of sky blue with white figures, collar, fan, and lace at neckline and sleeves. A white stocking and petticoat show above the blue slipper. A necklace matches the dress, and the bracelets are gold. The hat consists of a blue crown and feathers and a wide brim edged with blue.

Artistic Series III (No. 51) is another nine-inch blue-eyed blonde beauty with curly bangs and long curly tresses hanging loosely over her shoulders. She is dressed in white, with blue socks and black slippers.

Nine-inch blue-eyed blonde doll with curly bangs.

Costume III A is lavender, the dark parts of the illustrations deep plum color; revers, cuffs, buckle, bow and handle on parasol white. The hat matches.

No. III D is a beautiful shade of yellow with warm brown revers, cuffs and sash, white buttons and dickey. The hat is brown with a white feather and yellow ribbon just visible on the crown.

No. 52, Artistic Series 103, is the smallest Raphael Tuck "child" the writer has ever seen. It is five and one-half inches tall. A small owner of long ago has written on the back of this little blue-eyed blonde, "Helen, age 3 years." Helen's underwear is white with the exception of the bodice, which is pale blue to match her socks. Hair ribbon is white and the slippers tan with yellow and red pompons.

The dress shown (103) is greenish blue with green bertha and trimming, the green indicated by the shaded parts of the drawing. The hat matches. Yellow flowers on the hat match the butterfly pin stuck in the bow on the dress. The number of the doll is the number given all the costumes in this set. Two of the dresses, one yellow and white, one blue and white, are in the same style as No. 4 C, and Artistic Series No. 2 B.

Illustration No. 53, doll No. 501 in the series, twelve and one-half inches tall, is sketched with the costume 501 C in place. Underwear is similar to No. 103 except that the petticoat is blue and the waist white.

52

ARTISTIC SERIES
103

103

Artistic Series No. 103, exact size; the smallest Raphael Tuck
doll the author has ever seen.

Doll No. 501 in the Artistic Series, wearing outdoor costume (501-C), and with afternoon costume (501-D) shown at the right.

She is an angelic looking blonde with long curls. Her coat is foliage green with white polka dots, trimmed and lined with ermine except for the cape, which is lined with purple to match the dress. Muff and hat match, the latter trimmed with white plumes and purple ribbon. Stockings and gloves are warm brown and the slippers are black.

Costume 501A is typical of the 1894 period. It is a red dress trimmed with blue polka-dotted material, lapels lined with yellow to match yellow ribbons on the bag and a strip at either edge of the band at the hem line of the skirt. Stockings are black, gloves and shoes, brown, bachelor's buttons blue.

Over-trimming for children's wear was extreme in the gay nineties. In 501 B we have an example. The dress is white with a pink design. Ribbons and other parts shaded in the sketch are pink, lace and ruching white. A yellow parasol matches a straw hat, the latter trimmed with pink and red roses and bows.

Dress 501 D is a pale blue material figured in white to match the collar and sleeve ruffles and the edges of the dark blue ribbon trimming. The hat is corn colored straw trimmed with pale blue bows and white ostrich feathers.

Illustration No. 54, doll No. 503 in, the Series, is one of the rare brunettes. She has a profusion of black curls and her eyes are brown. She wears a pink petticoat and pink ribbon in her white chemise or corset cover, red stockings and slippers.

Additional costumes for Doll No. 501, the every-day dress at the left being typical of the 1894 period; at the right we see her walking costume, an example of the over-trimming for children's wear that was customary in the gay nineties.

At the left: Rare brunette doll, No. 503 of series, with her lavender and yellow costume shown at the right above.

Costume 503 A consists of a lavender skirt, cuffs and lower part of the waist. The waist is yellow with tan dots. Ribbon and band shown as black in the drawing are deep plum, the shaded part green and the unshaded, yellow.

No. 503 B is yellow with stripes of blue dots in the sleeves and an edge of same above the white lace ruffles at the bottom of the dress. The upper part of the dress also is trimmed with white lace, and a blue bow and necklace match the fan. The hat is the same shade of yellow as the dress, and is trimmed with white lace and a blue ribbon bow.

At left, yellow dress with stripes of blue dots in the sleeves, party costume for doll 503; and at right, walking outfit, red cape trimmed with black fur to match the muff and feathers on hat.

Outfit 503 C consists of a red cape trimmed with black fur to match the muff and feathers on the red hat, and a light gray pin-striped skirt with a black band around the bottom.

No. 503 D consists of a light blue dress and slippers, a white dotted Swiss apron, neck frill and sleeve trimmings, and a white hat trimmed with pale blue ribbons. The doll is dressed in yellow with dark blue stockings and shoes trimmed with red. A blue hair ribbon matches the blue eyes of the doll.

The small dress 101 is shown to illustrate the proportionate difference in sizes of the largest and smallest of the Raphael Tuck dolls in this Series.

Light blue playtime dress for doll 503, and white hat trimmed with pale blue ribbons. The small dress 101 at right is shown to illustrate the proportionate difference in sizes of the largest and smallest of the Raphael Tuck dolls in this series.

  The largest Raphael Tuck paper dolls the writer has seen are thirteen inches tall and are made to represent slender young girls rather than the child dolls just described. They are unnumbered and are made to stand with a cardboard easel, as are the other dolls described. Beside the Raphael Tuck trade mark, the easel and palette, printed on the back of the figure is the information:

  "Publishers by Appointment to Their Majesties The King and Queen Alexandra. Patd. Feb. 20th, 1894. Raphael Tuck & Sons, Ltd., London, Paris, Berlin, New York and Montreal. Designed at the Studios in New York and printed at the Fine Arts Works in Saxony."

  The heads of these dolls are printed separately and pasted onto an elongated neck. Again in this respect they are like the Artistic Series.

  Anne's elaborate underwear, (see illustration No. 55), consists of a white petticoat trimmed with white lace or embroidery and pink ribbon, and a pink corset cover trimmed with white ruffles and pink ribbon. She has brown eyes, stockings and slippers, and in her brown hair she wears a yellow ribbon rosette to match the yellow buckles on her slippers.

  The center costume *a*, is yellow with a white ruffle around the neck. In one hand is a blue fan decorated with pink flowers, and in the other a doll dressed in red with yellow dots, a white ruffle around the neck and sleeves to match the slippers and tan bands around the skirt. The doll's tam is blue and red striped and the slippers have red bows. Stockings are reddish brown.

The hat to go with this gown is a yellow straw, but the pale blue lining is most in evidence. It is trimmed with pink and white ostrich plumes and an orange ribbon bow.

Anne's garden costume at extreme left of the doll is pale gray with yellow bands around the bottom of the skirt and sleeve ruffles. The apron is white. Fichu and scarf are deep purple with yellow band trimmings. A yellow basket of cherries is tied at the wrist with green ribbon. The hat is yellow straw lined with purple silk to match the scarf and trimmed with purple and white violets, and a yellow pompon underneath the brim.

Anne, one of the Raphael Tuck paper dolls made to look like slender young girls rather than child dolls. She has brown eyes and brown hair, in which she wears a yellow ribbon rosette to match the yellow buckles on her slippers. Her every-day costume (a) has a white ruffle around the neck, the dress being yellow. She carries a blue fan decorated with pink flowers. The costume at the left is her garden apparel. It is pale gray with yellow bands around the bottom of the skirt and sleeve ruffles. The apron is white. the fichu and scarf are deep purple with yellow band trimmings, and she carries a yellow basket of cherries. (Name given for convenience).

56.

Sue.

**Sue, the little redhead in the Raphael Tuck "young girl" series.
She has blue eyes, wears a lavender bow in her hair. At the right
is her party dress of pale lavender. At left is a red play dress.
(Name given for convenience).**

"Sue" (No. 56) is a little redhead with blue eyes and lavender bows in
her hair. She wears a pale green dress figured with darker green, pale lavender
frill around the neck, and short puffed sleeves to match the frill; dark green
stockings and slippers; gold necklace and locket.

The party dress at right of the doll is a pale lavender with green ribbon
inserts and bows. Stockings and hat lining are a little darker shade of the same
color. Slippers match the dress, and the hat matches ribbons in the dress. Gloves
are cream color, bracelets, gold. One hand holds a white handkerchief, the
other a little red address booklet.

At the left of the doll is a red "play" dress trimmed with a white collar
and dickey, both collar and dickey edged with figured material in red and white.
There are three white bands around the bottom of the skirt. Buttons and spade
are yellow, and the pail is green.

Nancy, (No. 57) a blue-eyed blonde, wears a mauve dress with a white
shirred frill around the neck. Ribbons are magenta with matching rosettes on
slippers.

The outfit at right of the doll consists of a green and red plaid cape; shoes,
bag, skirt and trimmings, tan. A deep plum-colored ribbon with yellow bands
trims a yellow hat lined with shell pink.

Nancy, a blue-eyed blonde, who wears a mauve-colored dress with a white shirred frill around the neck. The ribbons are magenta. The school outfit at the right has a green and red plaid cape; the shoes, bag, skirt, and trimmings are tan. The semi-formal costume at the left is green with red trimmings, with a yellow collar which matches the yellow hat. (Name given for convenience).

The dress at left of the doll is green with red trimmings, and a broad yellow collar matching a yellow hat trimmed with yellow and red flowers.

Raphael Tuck dolls representing grown-ups seem to be far fewer than those representing children. Among the former are "The Belle of Newport, Blonde and Brunette Series of Dressing Dolls," and "The Bridal Party Series of Dressing Dolls." The figure in the cover design "Belle of Newport" illustrated is typical of this type of doll and her costumes.

Cover for "The Bridal Party," (a gold design on a gray background) does not illustrate the doll, but, through the courtesy of Mrs. Douse, we are able to reproduce not only the two cover designs, but "The Bridesmaid with Complete Outing Costumes" and the bridegroom with four separate suits and hat.

"The Bridesmaid," (No. 60) is Artistic Series No. 603, and is similar to the bride in the bridal set. She is a blonde with gray eyes. Her underwear consists of a white corset cover with cream colored ruffles and petticoat; ribbons in the corset cover, pink.

Costume 603 A is white with violet colored ribbon trimming to match the bouquet of violets in her hand and in the yellow straw hat.

Cover design of the "Belle of Newport" dolls.

58

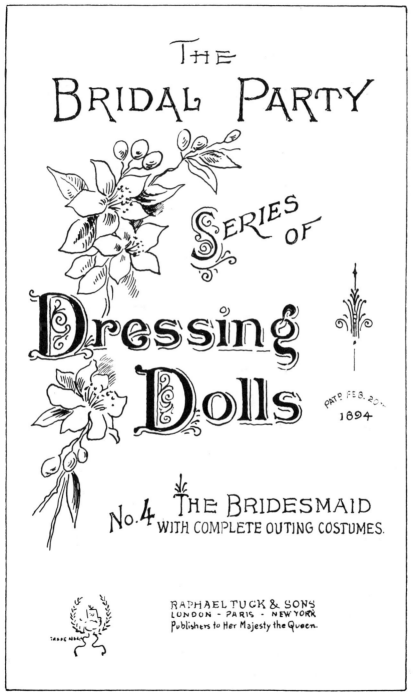

The

BRIDAL PARTY

Series of

Dressing Dolls

PAT⁰ FEB. 20ᵗʰ
1894

No. 4 THE BRIDESMAID
WITH COMPLETE OUTING COSTUMES.

RAPHAEL TUCK & SONS
LONDON - PARIS - NEW YORK
Publishers to Her Majesty the Queen.

59

Cover design for the "Bridal Party" Series.

"The Bridesmaid" in Artistic Series No. 603, with her boating and bicycling outfit.

Bridesmaid costume (A), and her walking costume (B).

Walking costume 603 B consists of a pale green and tan plaid skirt, and a tan jacket with gray trimming and feather boa. Hat matches the jacket and is profusely trimmed with gray ostrich feathers. Around the crown is green and tan striped ribbon. The little dog is white with black spots on head, ears and rump.

The boating outfit, 603 C, consists of a greenish-blue jumper trimmed with deep pink, matching the tie, and a white blouse with green pin stripes alternating with pink dots.

The bicycling costume (603 D) consists of a pastel plaid skirt in gray-green and pink, and a pink-striped blouse with white stock pencil-striped in gray; white cuffs, tan belt and gloves. The hat to go with this outfit is yellow straw trimmed with blue ribbon polka-dotted in white.

The nine and one-half-inch bridegroom (No. 61), is a little taller than his bride. He has brown hair, gray eyes, and wears a white blouse with blue tie and light blue trousers and stockings; tan shoes and belt.

Aside from the formal suit, *a*, the groom has a walking suit, *b*, consisting of a light tan jacket over a darker tan vest, gray trousers and white tie; a blue Service suit, *c*, with gold buttons and gold stripe on pants; and a lounging suit, *d*, the jacket plum color, pin-striped in red, and with yellow lapels; the pants gray-green plaid, and the shirt pale pink, pencil-striped in gray, and with a white tie.

Another interesting nine and one-half-inch Raphael Tuck doll owned by Mrs. Douse is "Little Janice," (No. 63), from *The Colonial Belles Series*. The doll and two of her four costumes with hats are illustrated, together with the cover design, No. 62, which came with this series. "Janice" has brown eyes and white hair, and wears a blue bodice trimmed with white, and a white petticoat trimmed with a tiny blue ruffle around the bottom. She has brown stockings and yellowish tan shoes.

The dress with panniers is yellow with pink flowers and green leaves, relieved by a white ruffle around neck and sleeves. The hat matches the dress. The costume at the right of the doll consists of a plum colored overdress with yellow revers and side trimmings, and a green skirt with pink flowers and vest. There are white ruffles underneath the revers and around the sleeves, and a plum colored ribbon band at the neck matches the ribbon in the yellow hat illustrated with the dress.

There seems to be no end to the list of Raphael Tuck paper dolls and cutouts. Miss Howard has in her possession two sets of cutouts with original envelopes, the sets beautifully designed and embossed, in full color, desirable alike to artist and student of history and costume design. One is a set of "the kings and queens of England from William the Conqueror to Queen Victoria, the entire series of thirty-seven rulers together with the Great Seal and coin of each respective reign comprised in thirteen sets of reliefs." The other set consists of the "soldiers of England from King Harold to Queen Victoria shown in a series of twenty-four representative armed warriors marking the different military epochs and comprised in twelve sheets of reliefs."

The "representative armed warriors" include a "Soldier of Harold, Bowman of William I, Spearman of William II, Knight of Stephen, Soldier of Henry

The Bridegroom and his formal attire (a); walking (b), military (c), and lounging (d) costumes.

62

Cover design for Little Janice, Colonial Belles Series.

63.

Janice.

"Little Janice" and two of her four costumes: Semi-formal (a); party (b).

II, Knight of Richard I, Banner Bearer of Edward I, Soldier of Richard II, Knight of Henry V, Knight of Henry VI, Crossbow man of Edward IV, Knight of Henry VII, Arquebusier of Henry VIII, Bowman of Elizabeth, Soldier of James I, Cavalier of Charles I, Pikeman of Cromwell, Musketeer of Charles II, Gentleman of the Guard of William III, Private of George II, Dragoon of George III, Infantryman of George IV, Lancer of William IV, and a Horse Guard of Queen Victoria.''

Three sets of the reliefs in question are illustrated here. See Nos. 64, 65 and 66. The figures in the reliefs are held together by seals, tabs, etc. The relief sketched at the top of the page consists of (left to right) Stephen, Henry II and Richard I together with seals and coins of the realm. The crown in each case is gold studded with jewels, and cushioned on the head with red velvet. Stephen wears red with blue sleeves showing and white lining in the oversleeves. Footwear is gold mesh with a touch of red at the instep. Henry II wears a red skirt with yellow dots in the cloth and trimmed around the bottom with bands of blue and gold between bands of white. His cloak is brown with gold trimming, and he wears black boots with red bands at ankle, attaching gold spurs. Richard I wears a white tunic trimmed with a red star, red belts and axe handle. His cloak is plum colored trimmed with gold to match the gold mesh leg and arm wear.

At lower left of the page are Harold's foot soldier and the bowman of

Three sets of reliefs in the "armed warrior" series: the English Kings Stephen, Henry II, and Richard I, at top. Lower left, foot soldier of King Harold, and bowman of William I. Lower right, Mary, wife of William III, and Queen Anne.

William I. The foot soldier carries a gold shield to match his headpiece and the color of his skirt. The upper part of the costume is blue over tan, leg and foot-wear tan. The bowman is dressed in gold armour, over which is a white tunic trimmed with bands of red.

The two queens, Mary, wife of William III, and Anne are brilliantly color-ful. Mary, the figure at the left, wears a red velvet overdress trimmed with ermine and decorated with gold and jewels with a touch of white at the neck and sleeve ruffles. Her brocaded skirt is in two tones of blue with a gold band at the bottom. She stands on a green carpet with designs in gold.

Anne wears a green dress with designs in the cloth of gold and pink, and the band at the bottom of the skirt is blue edged and decorated in gold. Her gold colored gloves match the golden ball in her hand, her girdle and golden ornaments. There is a touch of white at neck and sleeves, and both queens wear white slippers, and have varicolored jewels with pearls predominating. The carpet under Anne is red and one foot rests on a golden footstool.

It is too bad that the German blitz of World War II destroyed these beautiful plates. It would be difficult and costly to reproduce them as they were originally. We hope that eventually some of the sets will find their way to interested museums throughout the country so that an increasing number of students and collectors may have a chance to see them. They were made during the reign of Queen Victoria.

Chapter VIII

McLoughlin Brothers Paper Dolls

ONE of the oldest firms in America to publish children's books, paper toys and paper dolls was McLoughlin Brothers, referred to in Chapter III. Some of the latter bear the name of N. Orr Co., printed on the stand of the doll. This probably is the name of the engraver.

Among the earliest McLoughlin Brothers paper dolls to come to the attention of the writer is Susie, (No. 68), owned by Mrs. Douse. One dress belonging to this doll was in the Fawcett collection, and it was particularly gratifying to find in Mrs. Douse's collection not only Susie and four dresses, but the decorated envelope, (No. 67), in which she came. Susie, her envelope and two of the separate dresses are reproduced here through the courtesy of Mrs. Douse.

The cover design is in red, green and brown; spots on puppy, brown to match Susie's hair. The skirt is red and green plaid. This costume comes separately, but with different coloring—a green skirt and a lavender top trimmed with yellow banding around the hem of the frill.

Separate costumes illustrated are *a*, yellow with a white rabbit; *b*, two shades of pink with blue ribbons on shoulders, white lace sleeves and a yellow dove. The costumes are cut double with an opening at neckline, and they are printed both back and front. Another dress not shown is in blue and gray, and the "pet" in this case is a doll dressed in red.

The doll itself has light brown hair and shoes, a red rose in her hair from the bouquet in hand, and the heavier stripes in her stockings match the roses. Altogether she is a charming little six and one-half inch lady.

Another delightful early McLoughlin seven-inch paper doll with four separate dresses and bonnet was contributed by Miss Howard. A few months earlier Mrs. Eleanor Childs Vice-president of the Dollogy Club of Washington, D. C., had come forward with a McLoughlin envelope, (No. 69), picturing Ida May, the counterpart of Miss Howard's (until then) unidentified doll. The doll, (No. 70), four dresses and bonnet and the envelope are here illustrated. A note at the bottom of the envelope gives the year of publication. It reads "Entered according to Act of Congress, in the year 1858, by McLoughlin's Bro's, in the Clerk's Office of the District Court of the United States or Southern District of N. Y."

The dress marked *A* is a pale blue with darker blue dots, trimmed with white lace, and the flowers on the skirt are red, pink and yellow.

B is blue and white plaid with red and pink trimming over a white blouse.

Costume *C* is pale pink with darker pink bands around skirt and bodice, and pale green figured ribbon in broad bands down the length of skirt and waist. The rim and crown of bonnet are pale pink with darker pink stripes. A blue ribbon bow at back and front match a blue feather at left of bonnet. The right-hand feather is yellow. For contrast there is white ruching under the brim of the bonnet.

101

"Susie," product of McLoughlin Bros., two of her dresses, and envelope (67) in which she came.

Cover design for "Ida May," a McLoughlin Bros. paper doll of 1858.

"Ida May," with front and rear
views of her dresses for party
(a), and every-day (b).

Ida May's costumes for formal wear (c), and walking (d).

The outfit marked *D* consists of a dark blue coat trimmed with white fur collar; white blouse, and a blue-green skirt with darker tones of the same color in the trimmings.

Ida May herself has brown eyes and dark brown hair, the latter decorated with green rosettes and ribbon. Her underwear is untinted. Doll and costumes are printed both back and front, (Note illustrations). Dresses are pasted together at either side to allow slipping in place over the head of the figure.

Six-inch Alice, (No. 71), has all the earmarks of a McLoughlin paper doll, but the only name on the doll is Cogger or Cobber—the printing is indistinct— evidently the name of the artist. The name Alice is given for convenience. She seems to have been "born" in the 1860's. The doll has light brown hair, red lips and gaiters, and she stands on a green carpet. Both doll and costumes are printed back and front, the two sides pasted together on the edges so that, as in the case of Ida May, the dresses may slip over the head of the doll.

Alice, a doll of the 1860's, and her every-day dress with hat (a); walking costume and partial back view (b); afternoon dress (c); school dress (d); semi-formal costume (e).

Costume *A* is white, the skirt squared with blue lines. There are pink bows on the shoulders and a girdle of deeper pink. Accompanying the dress is a yellow straw hat trimmed with a blue feather and red about the crown.

The outfit marked *B* consists of a brown coat with black trimmings, over a blue skirt. A white sleeve is gathered at the wrist under the wide coat sleeve. The neck is finished with a red ribbon tied in a bow at the front. The cap, uncolored at the crown, is finished with a wide blue band and cocky blue feather.

C is in yellow with bands of light brown edged with white embroidery, over a white waist. The sash is plum colored with fringe of red.

D the plaid dress, has perpendicular stripes in red, parallel lines in red, the squares between, white. It is trimmed with bands of yellow edged with ruching of the same material.

The costume marked *E* is yellow ochre. A plum colored bodice shows beneath a light red or deep pink fichu. Diagonal stripes of pink ribbon edged with white ruching trim the skirt, and the same ruching trims the fichu, edges of bodice, and the sleeves. Light gray gloves complete the costume.

Kate, (No. 72), is another McLoughlin doll with the name given for convenience, and her period is also the 1860's. Her hair is light brown, and a little round pink ornament is caught up behind the ear, one visible at the left in front, one at each side at the back of the head. These ornaments match the gaiters. The doll stands on a foliage green carpet. Illustrations show the rear hairdo as

Kate, a name the author has selected as a matter of convenience, as in the case of Alice. She also seems to be of the period of the 1860's. Her hair is light brown, and she stands on green carpeting. Her costumes: walking dresses (a and b); calling costume (c); semi-formal dress (d); headgear (e).

well as the front of the doll. Sketches in circles illustrate the back of each costume only to the waist, since the skirt at the rear is exactly the same as it is in front.

Costume marked *A consists* of a blue and white checked skirt with trimming of brown puffed material, a brown jacket trimmed with black lace at the sleeves, and a white waist with collar showing. The bonnet shows a rim of tan, red roses and a large blue bow with white fringed edge.

B consists of a gray jacket trimmed with red, and a red skirt pin-striped in black with black bands at the hemline. A white blouse showing beneath the jacket is trimmed with red buttons at the cuff and a matching ornament at the throat. A green petticoat with design in black is revealed where the skirt is drawn up.

The jacket and under-skirt of *C* is plum colored, the former trimmed with black braid and buttons, the latter with two strips of white and an edge of black at the bottom. The overskirt is pale yellow with light brown stripes, and is held in puffs with buckles the same color as the jacket and skirt. A white collar, narrow white ruffles at the sleeves, and yellow gloves to match the skirt, complete the costume.

D is light gray with a white blouse and collar, and a dark blue girdle edged at the bottom with the same yellow trimming that appears on the sleeves and around the edge of the bolero. Fluting at the bottom of the skirt is the same except that it is edged with a strip of light brown. Yellow gloves match the dress trimming.

Back in the early 1860's McLoughlin Brothers also made portrait paper dolls. There was General Tom Thumb and his wee bride, Lavinia Warren, Lavinia's sister Minnie, who was the bridesmaid at the wedding, and Commodore Nut, the best man. This was a great event for the famous showman, P. T. Barnum, who featured the little people in his great exhibition. McLoughlin's

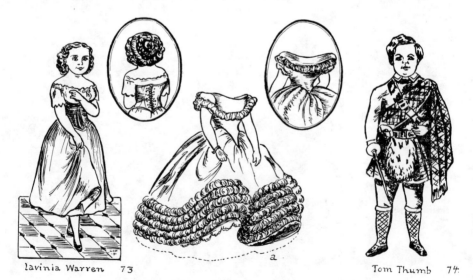

lavinia Warren   73   Tom Thumb   74

Lavinia Warren and Tom Thumb; her formal costume (a).

At top: "Little Eva," with costumes for walking (1) and afternoon (2). Below: "Baby," circa 1860, with sack (a), every-day dress (b).

also published Eugenia, Victoria and Carrie Grant at about the same time. Lavinia (No. 73) and "the General," (No. 74) are illustrated here.

"Little Eva," (No. 75) was a cut-out doll and therefore unmarked save for a pencil notation as to her name, but she has the earmarks of a McLoughlin doll of about 1860, and probably was meant to represent the well-known characters in Harriet Beecher Stowe's *Uncle Tom's Cabin,* for "Topsy" came with "Eva." Two of her three costumes are shown here. A third will be found on page 127 of *Dolls—A Guide for Collectors,* together with Eva's playmate. "Topsy." The doll is flesh tinted, her hair is brown, and her cerise shoes contrast with the green carpet on which she stands. Outfit No. 1 consists of a plum colored jacket trimmed with white fur and a light green skirt. The bow at the neckline matches the doll's shoes. Costume No. 2 is yellow with red trimming on the sleeves, red parasol, white ruching around the neck and light green gloves.

"Baby," (No. 76), also seems to be a McLoughlin doll of about the same period as Eva, and the tinting is the same except that she wears red socks and pale green bootees. The sack in costume *a* is tan embroidered in red and green; red tie and white collar, and the skirt is robin's egg blue. Costume *b* is reddish orange with blue trimmings over a white blouse.

Both the above mentioned dolls are three inches tall.

About 1875 McLoughlin Brothers appear to have gone into mass production. They printed quantities of penny leaflets and folders. One illustrated, in five parts, folded at dotted lines, shows Fanny and Pink on the outside cover of the fold, the dolls themselves with their costumes on the inside folds. (No. 77)

The kneeling figure on the cover has a red and white striped skirt, and a gray-blue bodice and peplum, trimmed with yellow bands on the upper sleeve, a ruffle of yellow around the peplum and a blue bow in yellow hair. The sitting child has a yellow dress shaded in red, with blue-green bands at neckline and upper sleeves and a white apron with blue-green band trimming and tie. She has a red ribbon in her dark hair. At the top the words are in red on a gray background. The name of the firm is in black.

"Pink" has a white petticoat or slip trimmed with a red band at top and bottom, white socks, red shoes and yellow hair. She stands on a rug with red diamond designs on a green background outlined with yellow. At the left of her is a yellow cap, above, a red dress with blue ruffles, and a yellow and green striped skirt, the smaller stripes green. The two dresses marked "Pink" are: left, a plum colored jacket trimmed with yellow; red bow; green polonaise; red skirt trimmed with yellow. The hat to go with this dress is red with a blue feather, the muff shaded in blue, and the gloves are yellow.

The costume at right consists of a yellow overdress trimmed with green ruffles, and a red skirt trimmed with blue ruffles. The hat is red with a white band.

"Fanny" also has yellow hair and white underwear. Her shoes are blue, and she stands on a mat of green, yellow, and red design. At the left of her is a red cap with white trimming. The dress above is blue-green with white bands, red ruffle and bows, left, a blue and red striped overdress and a yellow skirt trimmed with a red ruffle. A yellow hat at the left of this dress is trimmed with a blue-green band.

The costume at right consists of a red coat with ermine trimming and ermine muff, and a skirt of orange and yellow trimming. The hat is red with yellow trimming.

"Emily," (No. 78) came with a group of McLoughlin dolls of the 1870's. She has red hair, red spats over black boots, and stands on a carpet of yellow with designs in red. The dress at upper right of the doll consists of a yellow waist, which matches the wide yellow band at the bottom of the skirt, the main part of the latter in red and green stripes, and a red polonaise with yellow

McLoughlin Brothers Paper Dolls 111

A McLoughlin Bros. "penny leaflet" in five parts, showing Fanny and Pink. At right, top, we see Emily, and her afternoon costumes (a and b). At bottom right, cover design for Amelia, circa 1875.

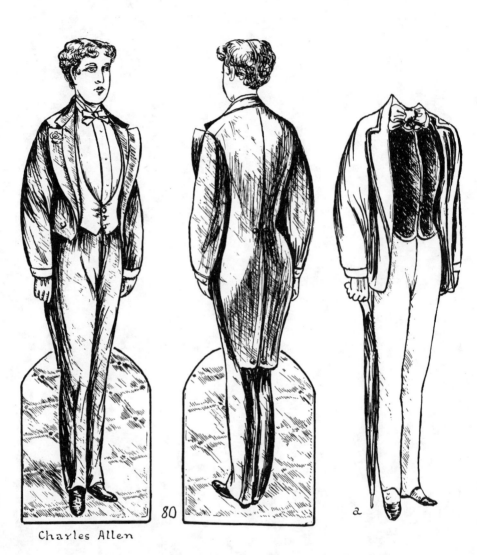

Charles Allen

Gentleman paper doll, groom in a bride and groom set published by McLoughlin Bros. about 1870.

flowers. The polonaise is edged with two black bands and a white ruffle. The latter matches the ruffles at neck and shoulders. Gloves are gray.

Emily's second costume consists of a green basque with yellow puffed sleeves to match the trimming at the edge of a green polonaise trimmed with red bows. The skirt is plum colored with yellow strips down the flounce. Clothes fit on by means of tabs.

"Amelia," (No. 79), looks so much like a McLoughlin doll that we illustrate it here for purposes of comparison. The back cover of the pamphlet on which Amelia appears bears the following: "Chromatic Printing Co., Philadelphia. Publishers of Toy-Books, Games, &c.

"Paper Dolls, 6 kinds. Bon Ton Series. Emily. Clara. Florence. Nellie. Amelia. Josephine.

"Paper Dolls, 6 kinds. 3 cents each. La Grand Series. Martha. Julia. Kate. Lucy. Clarissa. Minnie.

"Also, One-cent Dolls, Soldiers, &c. No. 1, 2, 3 and 4 Series, 6 kinds, 1 cent each."

"Amelia," reproduced through the courtesy of Mrs. Douse, is dressed in a green jacket and hat, a blue and red striped polonaise over a red skirt, shoes and feathers in hat to match the skirt, a white muff, and a blue and white striped blouse.

The original of the gentleman paper doll, (No. 80) is eight and one-half inches long, and is one of a pair, the only difference in them being that the mate to this "clean-shaven young man" has whiskers and "side-boards." He is untinted except for a pink tie and lips. One of his four costumes is shown with the doll. It consists of a dark red coat, black vest, gray trousers, blue tie, black shoes with white spats, tan gloves and a black umbrella. Doll and costumes are printed both back and front. It is the groom in a bride and groom set published by McLoughlin about 1870, and is the one referred to on page 126 of the author's *Dolls—A Guide for Collectors* as "Charles Allen, aged 26 years."

In the interesting booklet *Paper Dolls*, published by *The Newark, N. J., Museum*, written by Wilbur Macey Stone, the author states that McLoughlin paper dolls of about 1875 are inferior to the earlier ones, but less expensive. Mr. Stone speaks of finding McLoughlin dolls of 1899 "on sheets 8 by 12 inches, handsomely lithographed in full color, each doll with three dresses and hats to match and each sheet to retail at one cent! In 1900 they put out sheets of the dolls of all nations, of which I have, on one sheet, Scotland, Ireland and Wales, three costumes for one doll, Germany, Canada and Alsatia on another sheet and Japanese, Turk and American Indian on a third."

Chapter IX

Some Unidentified Dolls of 1870-1880

SOME years ago an elderly lady gave the writer a number of paper dolls. played with in the 1870's. These are colored on one side only, and the dresses are fastened onto the doll by means of tabs at shoulders and sides. The names given are those pencilled on the back of the figure so long ago that they are scarcely visible.

"Flora," (No. 81), is three and one-half inches high. She has brown eyes and hair. White underwear and gray stockings are trimmed with red, and she wears black slippers. The only touch of color in her otherwise light blue outfit *A* is in the hat, which is trimmed with a yellow band, red rosette and white bow. *B* is pink with red figures in the apron, the latter trimmed with white embroidery to match collar and cuff edgings. A larger doll like Flora is accompanied by a dress exactly like the one just described except that it is blue where the other is red. *C* is reddish gray with pale blue collar, bow and trimming. *D* is a tan coat over a red dress. Collar and tie, shoes and stockings also are red. The brim of the hat matches but the crown is brown.

"Marie," (No. 82), a brunette French nurse, is in two separate parts, back and front, the back attached to the front by means of tabs. This arrangement is true of the separate costume also. The doll itself holds a baby in a beautifully embroidered all-pink dress to match the color of the nurse's headgear. Marie wears a greenish-gray bodice like the skirt trimming seen in the rear view of the doll, and a gray and white striped apron over a blue-gray skirt; white stockings, black slippers, yellow ochre collar.

In the arms of the separate outfit is held a baby clad in white with blue bows. Bodice and skirt trimming of the figure are the same as those just described, but the skirt itself is red, the headgear white. The doll is four inches high.

"Miss Kate," (No. 83), and "Miss Lucy," (No. 84), also are four inches high. Kate is a brunette and wears red jewelry, a white corset cover, gray petticoat with darker gray trimming, and her shoes and stockings also are a darker gray. Miss Kate's housedress, *A*, is tan with brown collar and cuffs and skirt-band, and yellow trimmings at neck and cuffs; the apron white with red dots and bands. Her walking costume, with umbrella to match, is warm brown with darker brown collar and cuffs, and the blouse is yellow with red buttons. The evening gown, *C*, consists of an overdress of delft blue trimmed with yellow, and a yellow seven-flounced skirt. There are red roses at the point of bodice and shoulder.

"Miss Lucy" has light brown hair and slippers and white underwear. Her handsome evening gown, *D*, is red over a white skirt figured with pink and green flower sprays. Lace trimming is cream color and the flowers deep pink shading to light pink; gloves match lace. Lucy's walking costume is a lovely gray-green

114

Flora, a doll of the 1870's, with her afternoon dress and hat (a); apron dress (b); school dress and hat (c); every-day dress (d); winter walking costume (e).

Marie, a French nurse doll, with her change of costume (a).

the jacket in a little darker tone, probably meant to represent velvet. A white collar and pink tie make a nice touch of contrasting color. The afternoon dress, F is made of a pink striped material. It has a white bertha; trimmings and corsage, red. There are also red roses near the point of the basque.

At top, Miss Kate, a doll of the 1870's, with house dress (a); walking costume (b); formal dress (c). At bottom, Miss Lucy, also of the 1870's, with formal dress (d); walking costume (e); semi-formal frock (f).

Chapter X

A Family of Gay Nineties Paper Dolls

T HE gay nineties included in their gaiety a veritable deluge of paper dolls of all descriptions. Anyone who has been collecting paper dolls for any length of time realizes that it is from this period we draw the greatest number of old dolls. They range in quality from those printed on the cheapest paper in the cheapest manner possible to dolls printed on fine stock in full color. Among the latter is a family of 1895 paper dolls belonging to Mrs. Douse. The only printed identification are the initials "M. C. & K., 108 Times Building, New York City," and the year they were made. Six of the seven dolls, ("Grandfather" excluded), are reproduced here (Nos. 85-90). The bust of the doll which is separate (see sketch of boy) fits into the neckline of each costume, the latter double cut and hinged at the shoulders to allow a standing position. The arms fit around the garment at the front.

Mother   85

Father   86

Sister   87

Mother, Father, and Sister in the Gay Nineties set.

117

Baby   88.

Brother   89.

Grandmother.   90.

Baby, Brother, and Grandmother of the Gay Nineties set.

"Father" wears a dark gray coat and vest over his white shirt, light gray pants, black shoes, tie and top hat, tan gloves. A pink carnation in his lapel adds a touch of color. The eyes and hair are brown, moustache black.

"Mother" wears a tan dress with black lapels and neckband, tan gloves and hat, the latter trimmed with black and tan ribbon interspersed with red poppies; black shoes. She has light brown hair and blue-gray eyes.

"Sister" is very much overdressed. Skirt and lapels are blue trimmed with brown fur and braid respectively, and the blouse is white lace trimmed with brown fur. Sleeve cuffs are blue with a green bow. Her coloring is like that of her mother just described.

"Baby," whose coloring also is like her mother's, wears a yellow dress trimmed with white lace, the ruffle around her neck decorated with pink ribbon insertion, and a white bonnet.

Brown-haired, blue-eyed "Brother" wears a white, lace-trimmed blouse underneath his plum colored Eton jacket suit, the latter trimmed with yellow bands and buttons. A cap with yellow ribbon band and bow matches the suit. He has black slippers and white socks.

"Grandmother" is a white-haired, brown-eyed lady in lavender with white fichu edged with white lace to match the lace at bottom of skirt and sleeves, the fichu brought together at the bodice with a yellow bow. Her white cap is trimmed with a pale green bow, and yellow stockings show above her lavender slippers.

Chapter XI

Advertising Dolls

PAPER dolls used to advertise fashions, such as the old French fashion dolls, were perhaps the most beautiful and interesting. Charles Frederick Worth, a costume designer, made for his store a doll with fifty-five dresses and hats representing clothing from 1825 to 1895. The doll was mounted on tin and held upright in a wooden standard. Since then many department stores have used paper dolls to advertise the newest fabrics as well as the latest costume styles.

Much less impressive, but within the grasp of children of all stations in life were the "advertising" dolls which flooded the market during the 1890's and

Mr. Gardner and Mr. Fry, and their clothes.

120

Mrs. Mac, a McLaughlin Coffee advertising doll, and her walking outfit (a); afternoon dress (b); cape (c); skirt (d).

on into the twentieth century. They were launched by such firms as represented the McLaughlin, Cordova and Lion Coffees, New England Mince Meat, Aunt Jemima's Pancake Flour, Denison's Crepe Paper, Diamond Dyes, Clark's O. N. T. Spool Cotton, Hood's Preparations, Barbour's Irish Flax Threads and many others. Sometimes they came eight to sixteen in a set, and included men and boys as well as girls, women and babies, but usually only one doll was sent in exchange for each wrapper from the product in question, and a postage stamp or two to take care of mailing costs. Some came with double dotted lines on which to fold the doll so that it could stand; others folded to a sitting position; still others were made to stand by means of a doubled dress folded at the shoulders; some had separate skirts and waists which fitted together by means of tabs placed into slots. There were dolls with arms outstretched and others with arms close enough to the body so that a separate dress with arms attached could be fitted

Mary Queen of Scots, left; Marie Antoinette, right.

over the body of the doll. Many consisted only of head, arms and torso which had to be fitted into the costume to make the complete doll.

The greatest number and variety, judging from collectors' examples, were offered by McLaughlin's Coffee firm. The name should not be confused with McLoughlin Bros. Publishing Company, whose dolls already have been described in a previous chapter. The latter (still in existence) spells the name with an *o*, the former spelled it with an *a*.

"Mrs. Mac" (No. 91) is a typical housewife of 1894. Her blue dress with its white apron and neck ruffles makes a nice contrast to her rosy cheeks, blue eyes and red-brown hair. A dotted line at the bottom of the apron indicates a place to bend so that she may sit. This line also appears on her walking costume at right of the doll. The blouse comes separately and is made to fit into the skirt by means of a tab at the waistline of bodice fitting into a slot at the waistline of skirt. Shaded parts in the drawing indicate light green; unshaded parts, white; black parts indicate brown. The hat is green with white plumes.

The dress at lower left is the same cut as the one just described. It is pink with light brown trimming on the skirt, white lace on the waist, the latter trimmed at neck and waistline with red. A pink rose is carried in a white gloved hand.

The skirt at lower right is meant to be folded into pleats at dotted lines causing the doll to stand when it is in place. The cape, gray with yellow bands at the bottom, is fitted around the doll as indicated in the sketch. The skirt is a contrasting yellow ochre.

The gentlemen, "Mr. Gardner" (No. 92) and "Mr. Fry" (No. 93) were so named by a little one of long ago. "Mr. Gardner" is dressed in brown with a white shirt, black necktie and shoes. His separate suit is gray, the separate pants fitting into a slot just below the waistcoat. "Mr. Fry" is in typical evening clothes. His separate trousers, a yellowish gray, fit into a slot at his waistline, and the overcoat, brownish gray, fits over the head, as indicated.

McLaughlin's issued a great many dolls of this general type during the 1890's. Many of them read on the reverse side: "To make the doll sit, bend on heavy lines. To make the doll stand, bend on dotted lines. One doll, consisting of doll, extra garment, hat and piece of furniture, in each package." Lines referred to were on the reverse side of the doll. Also on the reverse side of the women and girl dolls was the following advertisement: "McLaughlins Coffee is better quality than any other package Coffee in the market. This is the reason why it has such an enormous sale. One complete doll in each package." The name and address of the dealer followed. Advertising on the back of the men dolls includes the information "8 men and 8 women dolls in this set."

One of the most interesting sets published by McLaughlin's was the set of famous queens. On the reverse side of the "queens" is a picture "in small" of a piece of furniture which came with the figure together with instructions for setting up.

The doll representing **Mary, Queen of Scots** (No. 94) wears a deep pink overdress lined with pale green. The skirt is a yellow brocade, the waist white. The Crown is gold over a pale lavender puff. She has brown eyes and grayish brown hair.

"Marie Antoinette" (No. 95) is dressed in white—alas!—for the guillotine! She wears a black band in her white cap, black shows at the neckline. and her slippers and stockings are black. Eyes are brown, hair white, presumably powdered.

"Queen Isabella" (No. 96) wears a robin's egg blue overdress, the oversleeves lined with ermine, and the skirt is white with gold colored trimming, and alternate pearls and rubies down the center and at the bosom. The lower part of the sleeves have alternate stripes in blue and white, edged with gold color. Girdle and sleeve ruffles are white. She is represented as a brunette.

Isabella's separate costume, a, is white with gold and red designs in the oversleeves to match the gold and red trimmings and the jewelry in the front of the bodice.

The McLaughlin Coffee Dolls of 1894, two boys and a girl, each with separate costume, are reproduced here through the courtesy of Miss Howard. Figure No. 97 is a blonde boy with blue eyes. He wears a pink and white striped blouse with

96.   a.

Queen Isabella of Spain, and her court costume (a).

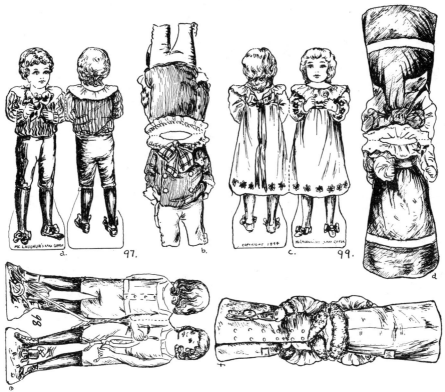

McLaughlin Coffee dolls; boy (97) and separate costume (b); another boy (98) and overcoat (f); girl (99) and costume (d).

white collar and red plaid tie, short green pants, black stockings and slippers, the latter with enormous bows. His extra costume, *b,* boasts a light tan striped blouse with darker tan pin stripes, yellow buttons, white collar and cuffs and white trousers.

The little girl, No. 99, is another blonde with blue eyes. Her dress is white trimmed with red flowers to match red bows on her gray slippers. Stockings also are gray. Costume *d* is lavender with white sleeves, white ruffle at neckline and band on skirt. In the hand is a pink and red pinwheel.

Doll No. 98 also is a blonde. His overcoat, *f,* is green with brown fur trimming; accessories, a yellow scarf and red mittens.

All these dolls fold at the side and stand by opening out as one does a screen. It will be seen that both doll and costume are printed back and front, and the costume is added by inserting head in the opening at neckline.

"Bunny" (No. 100) is another McLaughlin Coffee doll which folds at the side. Underwear is white with a tan petticoat, stockings blue with tan dots, slippers brown, and the rabbits are white. The girl has blue eyes and light hair. Her separate coat costume, *a,* is cream color with a white dress showing. The toy is striped in red and white. Hat marked *b* at left of the costume is white trimmed with a yellow ribbon bow; the other, *c,* at left of the doll, is a yellow straw trimmed with brown ribbon.

The 1892 Palmer Cox Brownie, (No. 101) comes in two parts, a blue-eyed head with a long tab under the chin, which fits into a separate body by means of two slits for the tab to enter, one at the neck and one at the waistline. The Brownie has a short red jacket over yellow trousers, black stockings and a black hat, the latter trimmed with a yellow band near the edge of the brim and a red, white and blue circle in the center of the brim. Base folds back at either side to make the figure stand. It was used to advertise Lion Coffee.

Blonde "Little Bo Peep" (No. 102) is dressed in the conventional white underwear with blue ribbon bands at neckline and sleeves, white stockings, blue slippers; and a pink bonnet matches small pompons on her slippers. Her separate costume, d, is pink with white collar and gold colored trimming on her skirt. The lamb is white with a blue bow. Printing on the inside cover of the dress reads: "Capital Coffee is the strongest, purest and best you can buy. Examine carefully the list of premiums we offer for the return of wrappers. Save yours and forward to The Ohio Coffee and Spice Co., Columbus, O., U. S. A."

"Flo" (No. 103) is a blonde early twentieth century paper doll last issued in 1915 by the Loose-Wiles Biscuit Co. On the reverse side of the doll is printed:

"Dresses, coats, hats, etc. for this doll will be found in the following packages of Sunshine Biscuits. MORNING DRESS AND HAT in 5c Sunshine Yum-yums and 25c Sunshine (here printing is erased) PARTY DRESS AND HEAD GEAR in 10c Sunshine Graham Crackers." etc.

The doll's white underwear is typical of children's wear in the early years of this century. She has warm orange-tan shoes and stockings, which match the suit e, at upper right of the doll. The latter is trimmed with brown collar, cuffs and belt and gray buttons. The coat and muff f, are black representing fur, and the coat is trimmed with white fur.

While most of the nineteenth century advertising dolls collectors are able to find come from the period of the 1890's, one occasionally finds an earlier example, such as "Cora," (No. 104) named after the present owner, Mrs. Cora Lake of Livingston, Montana, through whose courtesy the doll is sketched. "Cora" advertises the Duplex Corsets patented in 1875. The doll has brown eyes and hair, white corset, petticoat and stockings; brown slippers, yellow necklace, and on her ribbon hair band is printed the name "Duplex Corsets." Over the opening at the hip is the information "No bones over the hips to break." The tab at this point gives the patent date under the word "Adjustable." Beneath the corset are the words "I wear the" and the trade mark with the name is given.

In the early days even Spalding's Sporting Goods Company advertised through paper doll cutouts. One of their football heroes, "Tom," (No. 105) is illustrated here. He is a brunette and wears a gray uniform with blue shirt and brown sports shoes.

Worcester Salt Company advertised through nursery rhyme cutout dolls, such as "Little Jack Horner" (No. 106) seen in the sketch. He has gray eyes and brown hair and wears a light blue shirt with white collar, yellow tie, mauve trousers, white stockings and black slippers. The stool is green and the flooring a brownish pink. The latter folds back at dotted lines to make a stand.

McLaughlin child with rabbit (100), and separate costume (a); hat (b); another hat (c);
Palmer Cox Brownie of 1892 (101); Little Bo Peep (102) and costume with lamb (d); Flo
(103), a Loose Wiles Biscuit Co. doll of 1915, with her spring outfit (e); winter outfit (f).

I WEAR THE DUPLEX CORSET

104.   Cora

Cora, advertising Duplex corsets, patented in 1875, separate costume (a).

At left, Spalding's football hero "Tom"; center, "Jack Horner," advertising for the Worcester Salt. Co.; at right "Olympia," the Wheeler and Wilson sewing machine girl.

The blonde, blue-eyed sewing machine girl (No. 107) was offered by the Wilson Sewing Machine Company. She is clad in yellow with pink collar, cuffs and tie and brown stockings and shoes. These three dolls also were contributed by Mrs. Lake.

One of the joys of paper doll collecting is that friends are always willing to cooperate. The little O. N. T. Bride and Groom, Nos 108 and 109 respectively, came to the author from a friend in Columbus, Ohio, Mrs. Raymond P. Baker, who, in turn, received it from one who was doing her spring housecleaning. "Marie" and "Raymond" look rather young to be taking such a serious step in life. But this marriage of the paper dolls has been going on for more than fifty years, and neither of them are much the worse for wear. They will now join company with a box of their kind purchased in Maine last summer while the author was "antiquing."

"Antiquing" is a delightful pastime. One never knows on pausing before some intriguing village antique shop just what is behind its magic doors. The writer was looking for paper dolls in a Maine village the summer of 1949 when she came to a particularly promising farm house on the lawn of which, in front of a barn, all sorts of remnants of the past were strewn about. In answer to the query "I don't suppose you have any paper dolls?" came the reply, "No, not here, but my wife has a box full of them, pretty ones, too. I will 'phone her to bring them over. We live only two miles away."

The box contained dozens of Clark's O. N. T. Spool Cotton advertising dolls of the 1800's, and a few extolling the virtues of Enameline Stove Polish. Names accompanying them were in a child's hand-writing on the back of the dolls.

108.   109.

O.N.T. BRIDE and GROOM
Marie   Raymond

The O.N.T. bride and groom, Marie and Raymond.

"Amelia" (No. 110) must have been among the earliest of the Clark dolls, for she does not bear the trade mark at the back of the head, as do the others, although her head and arms fit into the costume in the same manner, the head slipped through the opening at the neck of the double-cut outfit, the arms brought forward over the dress. On the back of the fold is the advertising "CLARK'S O. N. T. SPOOL COTTON IS THE BEST FOR HAND AND MACHINE SEWING." On the inner cover is the information that there are sixteen dolls in each set, which may be obtained by sending three two-cent stamps to George A. Clark & Brother, 400 Broadway, New York City.

"Amelia" is a dark-haired miss with eyes to match her robin's egg blue dress, the later trimmed with white ruffles and jabot. The under brim of her yellow straw hat is decorated with purple ribbon pompons, and the trimming, tie and feathers are of the same color.

A number of these dolls are evidently playing "Mamma," for there are spectacles balanced halfway down their chubby wee noses, and they carry symbols of household chores, such as broom and dustpan, sewing materials, etc. Blonde, blue-eyed "Etta" (No. 111) is playing "Mother," for she carries a doll. Her dress is yellow with white cuffs, and she wears a white apron and cap, the latter trimmed with a blue bow. The hair of her doll matches her own, and the dress is white with a yellow ribbon.

"Baby Lena" (No. 112) wears a pinkish white dress with lavender ribbon sash. The white of her cap scarcely shows beneath voluminous pink ribbons. Bonnet tie is also pink. "Lena" has brown eyes and hair.

Raymond, Phillip and *Ralph*, also Clark dolls, show what the well-dressed little boy of 1895 looked like. Raymond's suit is lavender-pink with yellow cuffs and a yellow and white striped tie. His hat is green, a nice contrast to his red hair and lovely brown eyes.

Phillip's suit probably is meant to represent velvet. His white neck and sleeve ruffles, tie and sash and black Mary-Jane slippers make him resemble

Amelia, Etta, and Lena, advertising O.N.T. spool cotton.

Raymond *113*   Phillip *114.*   Ralph *115.*

Raymond, Phillip, and Ralph, Clark's O.N.T. boys.

Little Lord Fauntleroy. A yellow straw hat matches his hair. The innocence of childhood shines in his wide blue eyes.

"Ralph" wears a swagger Eton jacket of deep purplish velvet trimmed with tiny white buttons, the cuffs, neck ruffle and tie of his white blouse showing. His plaid pleated skirt and hat-band carry out the color scheme of his blouse and jacket. The cap is black trimmed with a white rosette, and the stockings and slippers are black.

Dolls advertising Enameline Stove Polish also were in the box referred to above. Three of these *John, Kathryn* and *George,* are typical examples. They differ from the Clark Dolls in that they are all in one piece. While they fold at the shoulders in the same way, the head is cut out from the back piece, so that it remains in position when the fold is made at the shoulders to enable the doll to stand. The name ENAMELINE is stamped either on the belt or the athletic equipment the doll is carrying. Printed matter on the back of the fold explains that these are college color dolls and a set of nine representing different colleges will be mailed upon receipt of two two-cent stamps and three top labels taken from boxes of Enameline. Underneath, boxed in red letters, is the explanation that John is a Yale University man, Kathryn a Bryn Mawr College lassie, and George a Yale University athlete. They must have been infant prodigies, for each appears to be about six years old. Advertising on the inside covers of the dolls extolls the virtues of Enameline and warns the public not to buy other brands that cannot possibly match the marvelous qualities of Enameline, the old line that still is used.

"John" is a brunette with red sweater, white letter and white trousers and socks and pale green sports shoes. "Kathryn" also is a brunette, but with blue eyes. Her blouse is canary yellow trimmed with black bands at the throat. She wears a white skirt, black stocking and white sports shoes trimmed with brown, very much like modern shoes. "George" is a real blond. His sweater and stockings are blue, knickers and shoes, gray. The letter Y is white.

How different now must be the little hands that fondled these dolls so long ago in a world of make-believe. They probably have done and may still be doing useful work in the larger world of reality.

The uncut paper dolls "presented by The Willimantic Thread Co." are illustrated here through the courtesy of Miss Howard. These came in folders with the directions: "Cut out the figure, garments, etc., following the outlines, being careful to preserve the small projections on each, indicated by dotted lines. These, folded backward, serve to hold the different garments on figure when properly adjusted. The figure may be attached to a small block of wood, so it can be stood upright." A clue to the date it was printed is given in the information that it was given "highest awards at N. O. Exhibition 1885."

The girl doll, a brunette, (No. 119), is clad in white underwear with pink shoulder straps, white socks and brown shoes. Socks indicate a child under seven years of age, for no self-respecting girl over six would wear socks in 1885; modesty forbade. The coat is light green with darker green trimming and

John, Kathryn, and George, advertising Enameline.

gloves. A red dress shows underneath, and the smaller collar at neck is red. Tan leggings match the muff. A green bonnet is lined with red to match the ribbon and tie, and the same color scheme is carried out in the blanket roll. At right of the fold, which is indicated by the dotted line, are three dresses, accessories and playthings. The upper left-hand dress is in two shades of pink, and a pink string bag goes with the outfit. At upper right is a blue dress with white trimmings, and below it, a grayish tan dress is trimmed with a red sash and red bows on the shoulders. The doll is dressed in blue with red trimmings, and the bag at the left of the doll is green with red tassels and pink flower embroidery.

The "Williamantic boy" (No. 120) also a brunette, is clad in a white blouse with gray trimming and tie, gray pants and stockings and black shoes. His extra coat and suit on the same side of the folder are green with light blue trimming. The tie, collar and cuffs are trimmed with white braid. A butterfly net at the top of the right side of the folder, and the white kite with red tassels and varicolored feathers, seem to go with the play suit at upper right. The latter is light green with darker green collar and lapel. The military uniform consists of a red jacket and black trousers and boots, the entire costume trimmed with narrow bands of white. The overcoat is tan with dark collar, red scarf and

THE WILLIMANTIC THREAD CO.

PRESENTED BY

119

Brunette doll presented by the Willimantic Thread Company.

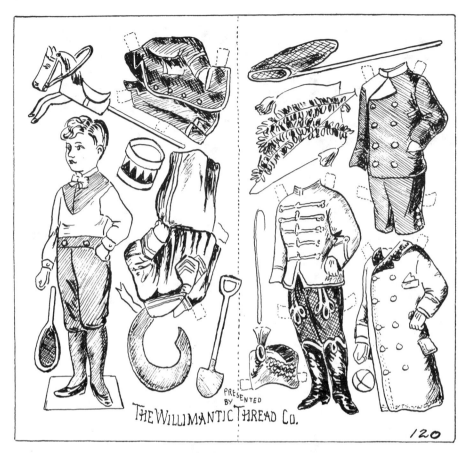

The Willimantic Thread Company's boy, also a brunette. His wardrobe includes a military
uniform and a play suit, and some of his playthings are included in the cut-out.

handkerchief and white cuffs showing. The cap is tan with a red crown, and
the ball blue and red. These are four-inch dolls.

Among the largest and most pretentious of the advertising dolls are those
presented by C. I. Hood & Co., who dealt in sarsaparilla, pills and tooth paste.
The set, owned by Mrs. Douse, consists of five dolls, four of which are illustrated
here—Pa (No. 121), Ma (No. 122), Brother (No. 123), and Sister (No. 124),
each with separate costume which fits on the doll by means of tabs inserted
in slots underneath the hair or frill as the case might be.

The little girl, a seven-inch blue-eyed blonde with gray stockings and yellow
slippers trimmed with blue bows, seems to be the forerunner of the set. Advertising on the front of the doll reads:

"I am one of Hood's Paper Dolls. There are five of us, Pa and Ma, Sister
and Brother and Me. We have plenty of good clothes, 19 pieces in all, for full
particulars how to get the whole family, see other side. C. I. Hood & Co., Lowell,
Mass. Copyrighted 1894, Patent Applied For."

C. I. Hood & Co. family of paper dolls.

The reverse side of the doll reads:

"Hood's Paper Dolls are right up to date. Largest, handsomest, most complete set ever issued. They are lithographed in beautiful colors, strongly made of heavy manila paper, and are exquisite in every respect.

"They are all cut out and are not sent in sheets like other dolls which have to be cut out and pasted together and which you are reasonably sure to spoil before you get anywhere near into shape. Hood's Dolls are all ready for use the minute you get them, and the dressing and changing of clothes will amuse the children for hours. They will also stand alone, and thus make neat mantle or boudoir ornaments.

"The Doll of which this is a sample is one of the smallest in the set. Thus they are unusually large and are fully equal to dolls sold in the stores for 50 cents or more.

"How to Obtain Hood's Dolls.

"These Dolls are issued complimentary to patrons of Hood's Pills and will be sent to any address on receipt of 10 cents in stamps and one trade-mark from Hood's Pills. They cannot be secured in any other way. Write your address plainly and send trade-mark and stamps to C. I. Hood & Co., Lowell, Mass., U. S. A.

"In Great Britain send 5d. and trade-mark to C. I. Hood & Co., 34, Snow Hill, London, E. C."

"Sister" is accompanied by a pink dress with white lace and black ribbon trimming and bow. Her straw hat is pale pink trimmed with a black ribbon band and decorated with pink roses, a pink and blue feather, and lace ruffles in tan and white.

"Brother" advertises Hood's Sarsaparilla "which will purify and vitalize the blood, give strength and appetite and produce sweet and refreshing sleep," according to the promise on the reverse side of the doll. He is an attractive seven-inch doll with dark brown hair, blue eyes, straw stationery hat, white underwear with pink ribbon at neckline, blue socks striped with tan, and black slippers. Printing on shirt reads "cut through the card on heavy black outlines of hair." His sailor suit is medium blue with light blue collar, yellow stars and buttons, and black slippers.

Nine-inch "Pa," is quite a fellow with his long white underwear, "sideboards" and moustache. Printing on his chest is the same as that on the boy's underwear except that the word "whiskers" is substituted for "hair." On the reverse side he also praises the wonders of Hood's Sarsaparilla. Separate costume consists of a black coat, white and tan pin-striped trousers, blue vest polka dotted in white, black tie with white shirt, gold watch chain and a pink carnation. He has blue eyes and light brown hair, moustache and beard.

"Ma" has light brown hair and hazel eyes. Her vest or corset cover is robin's egg blue trimmed with white lace. Printing on front of vest reads: "Cut through ruffle on heavy black outlines." The lady's petticoat is black with a two-toned blue-edged ruffle finished with white lace. She wears black stockings, and her brown slippers match the hat. The latter is trimmed with a green bow and blue feathers. Printing on the reverse side of the doll credits Hood's Sarsaparilla for good effects on the nerves, and concludes with the statement: "Therefore the true way to cure all nervous troubles is to feed the nerves upon pure blood; and to make the blood pure, rich and healthful, there is no remedy equal to Hood's Sarsaparilla." The admonition to use this "blood and nerve" medicine is continued on the reverse side of the separate dress shown in the illustration. This costume shows the "kangaroo" shape at its worst. The Eton jacket and skirt are gray trimmed with darker gray braid. Revers are blue, and the umbrella orange-pink with white lace ruffles.

Advertising dolls tell something of human history—invention, medicine, food, clothing, etc., and they have brought much happiness to children of the past who had few of the advantages offered today's children even in the humblest of homes.

Chapter XII

Activated Paper Dolls

THE beginnings of action paper dolls have been touched upon in the chapter dealing with paper doll history. As stated before, the ideas for motion paper dolls goes back as far as early Egyptian times.

In the files of the United States Patent Office, Washington, D. C., are a number of papers granting patents for motion paper dolls to various persons. Reproduced here are the drawings which accompanied the one granted Wm. H. Hart, Jr., of Philadelphia, Pa., Dec. 1, 1874 (No. 125).

A more recent "walking" paper doll, copyrighted in 1920 by Daddy Long Legs, U. S. Toy Corporation, New York, N. Y., shows a rotating wheel of five legs fastened between a two-piece cardboard figure, one showing the front of the doll, the other the back view. Wedged between the two pieces, above the rotating wheel of legs, is a socket for the insertion of a stick to facilitate handling. As the doll is propelled, only one pair of legs is visible at a time, as was the case with a real walking doll fifty years earlier.

Of recent years a small but fascinating shop, Burtons of Sixth Avenue, New York, devoted to old prints, magazines, etc., put on sale a number of swinging-limbed paper dolls patented in 1880. The illustrations showing two of the early actresses, one assembled, and one unassembled, came from this shop. When put together, which is done with brass fasteners, they are fourteen inches high. The two darky dolls and the Indians, one of the latter unassembled, also came from this shop. They are all in full color, and are nine inches high.

The company best known for selling this type of doll in America is the Dennison Manufacturing Company, which has places of business in New York, Boston, Philadelphia, Chicago, Cincinnati and St. Louis. Most, if not all of the dolls marked MM in the illustrations, from the collection of Mrs. Mary Mallon of Philadelphia, Pa., and the one named Corala, from Mrs. Lake's collection, were sold originally through the Dennison Manufacturing Company, as evidenced through old catalogs of the firm. One such, called "Art and Decoration in Crepe and Tissue Paper," copyrighted in 1902, is in the possession of Mrs. Willie H. Armstrong, of Austin, Texas. Judging from the dress styles in the old catalog, which is undated, the swinging arms and legs dolls shown here were presented about 1894 by Dennison's fourteen years after the patent date but they are mentioned in a much earlier catalog. Some of the dolls illustrated are referred to in this catalog under the title "Jointed Dolls," from which the following quotation is taken:

"To the line of lithographed dolls' heads has been recently added a new patented style complete in all parts; that is, with head and limbs attached to a body form. The arms and legs are movable, being jointed with eyelets as shown in the cut. These jointed dolls are made in five sizes, two of children and three of ballet dancers, and can be had with or without dresses. (See price list.) We show three or four styles of these dressed in Crepe Paper which, when seen, are hailed with delight by the little mothers who are particularly pleased because of the movable arms and legs and the truly artistic costumes to be obtained from crepe paper. The jointed forms are easily dressed with crepe paper at small expense, and as something entirely new and novel in the doll line are unsurpassed. It will now be

**Swinging-limbed paper dolls, one assembled and one
unassembled, which came from Burton's, New York.**

UNITED STATES PATENT OFFICE.

WILLIAM H. HART, JR., OF PHILADELPHIA, PENNSYLVANIA.

IMPROVEMENT IN DOLLS.

Specification forming part of Letters Patent No. **157,394,** dated December 1, 1874 ; application filed October 31, 1874.

To all whom it may concern:

Be it known that I, WILLIAM H. HART, Jr., of the city and county of Philadelphia, and the State of Pennsylvania, have invented a new and useful Improvement in Dolls and Wardrobe therefor; and I do hereby declare the following to be a clear and exact description of the nature thereof, sufficient to enable others skilled in the art to which my invention appertains to fully understand, make, and use the same, reference being had to the accompanying drawings making part of this specification, in which—

Figure 1 is a general view of the device embodying my invention. Fig. 2 is a vertical section thereof in line *x x*, Fig. 1. Fig. 3 is a view of Fig. 1, certain parts being removed. Figs. 4 and 5 are views of detached parts. Fig. 6 is a bottom view.

Similar letters of reference indicate corresponding parts in the several figures.

My invention consists in constructing the body of a doll of separated parts or sections, whereby they may be fitted to various dresses. It also consists in providing the parts of the doll and the dress with tongues and pockets, whereby said parts and dress may be nicely and securely fitted to each other. It further consists in so constructing the doll that it may be made to oscillate and assume the appearance of walking.

Referring to the drawings, A represents a doll, whose body is constructed of the head portion B, legs C, and trunk D, which are separated from each other. E E′ represent tongues, which are formed on the head B and legs C at ends thereof, adjacent to the trunk D, and in said trunk D there are formed vertically-extending pockets F, into which tongues E E′ of the head and legs are adapted to enter and be held. G represents the doll's dress, which is open at top and bottom, and within the same is secured the trunk D.

It will be seen that the head and legs of the doll may be readily applied to the trunk D, and thus complete or build up the doll, as seen in Fig. 2. Should a different dress be required, the head and legs are removed and applied to the trunk having the proper dress thereon. If different-colored shoes are required, the legs having the desired colored shoes will be applied in lieu of those occupying the trunk.

In fact, various changes may be made to suit the taste or whim of the child owning the doll.

It is evident that the arms H and portion J of the garment corresponding to a sack, basque, or overskirt, may be provided with tongues, and thus adapted to be applied to and removed from the trunk D, whereby variety in dressing the doll will be increased.

The trunk D will be secured to and suspended from the upper end of the dress by means of a link, staple, wire, or other fastening, K, and thus vibrate freely on said fastening K. A finger-piece or lever, L, is secured to the trunk D, and projects laterally therefrom through an opening, M, in the rear or rear piece N of the dress G.

It will be seen that by holding the dress by one hand, and reciprocating the finger-piece L, the trunk will be vibrated, and thus impart a vibrating or oscillating motion to the head and legs of the doll, whereby the movements of walking will be readily imitated.

If desired, the weak parts of the trunk and portion of the dress at the fastening K may be strengthened with strips of muslin or other suitable re-enforcing material.

Having thus described my invention, what I claim as new, and desire to secure by Letters Patent, is—

1. The doll A, having its body B C D composed of separate sections, constructed and arranged substantially as and for the purpose set forth.

2. The doll-sections B C, formed with tongues E E′, in combination with the trunk D, provided with pockets F, substantially as and for the purpose set forth.

3. The combination, with the doll-dress G, of the oscillating trunk D, suspended therein by means of the fastening K, which constitutes the axis of the trunk, substantially as and for the purpose set forth.

4. The oscillating trunk D and operating finger-piece or lever L, combined and arranged to operate substantially as and for the purpose set forth.

WM. H. HART, JR.

Witnesses:
JOHN A. WIEDERSHEIM,
A. P. GRANT.

Patent granted William H. Hart, Jr., for improvement in dolls.
(Illustrated on opposite page).

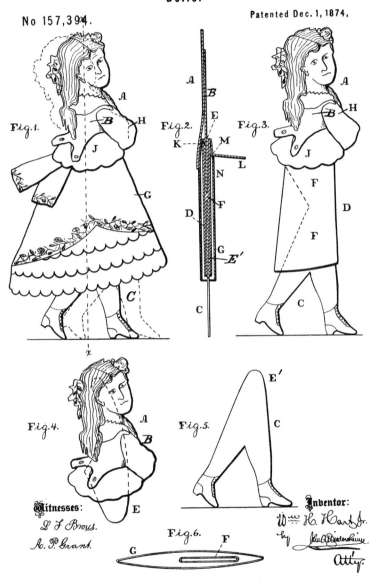

W. H. HART, Jr.

Dolls.

No 157,394.   Patented Dec. 1, 1874.

Fig.1.

Fig.2.

Fig.3.

Fig.4.

Fig.5.

Witnesses:
L. F. Brous.
A. P. Grant.

Fig.6.

Inventor:
Wm. H. Hart Jr.
by
John A. Diedensheim
Atty.

THE GRAPHIC CO. PHOTO-LITH 39 & 41 PARK PLACE, N.Y.

Illustration No. 125—Drawings which accompanied the patent
granted W. H. Hart, Jr., shown on opposite page.

possible for every child to have a family of fine appearing and exquisite dolls. Directions for making the costumes of those illustrated are as follows:

"For the smallest one, jointed form No. 2 was used. A piece of white crepe paper one-half yard in width and three and one-half inches in length, was cut on the length of the paper. This was finely gathered at the top and tied about the waist of the doll and fastened by sewing in and out through the body. The open sides were then glued together. Another similar piece of white, the same width, but only three inches in length, was placed over this and fastened in the same way, forming a double skirt. The lower edges of the skirt were then pulled out between the fingers and the upper skirt being the shorter, is gracefully looped up and caught down with gold stars, while a row of stars also ornament the under skirt. (For gold stars in sheets see page 56.) A ruffle about an inch deep and a couple of inches long is glued on the neck in front (not any in the back) and then turned neatly over and pressed firmly down, and the little dress is finished. Now take a piece of ruby crepe six inches in width, cut on the length of the crepe, and three inches in depth, turn up a narrow hem on the bottom and a wider one on the front edges, shape the neck and shoulders and slant the fronts off into points which when turned back form revers; cut the sleeves two inches in length, shape them at the wrist and pull out at the shoulders, glue these into the arm holes and you have your little jacket complete. Cut your cap out of a small square of stiff paper, covered with red crepe and glued to the head by a narrow band of crepe. Place some gold stars about the collar of the jacket and one at the end of each rever, and your little maiden is complete.

Swinging-limbed Indians bought at Burton's, New York.

127

Darky dolls acquired from Burton's, New York.

"The costume of No. 1 doll was fashioned thus: Her underskirt of white is cut the same as that of her younger sister, only longer, four and one-half inches long and three-quarters of a yard wide. The outer skirt of pink is similar and both are fastened on as described above. A straight piece of white crepe is fastened about the waist, the neck being cut low and the arm holes cut out. A long band of baby ribbon is placed about the waist, concealing the joining of the skirt and waist and bowed in front. Small pieces of the white are then cut on the circle gathered at both ends, slipped on the arms and fastened at the shoulders. These also have bands of ribbon bowed at the elbow. And now for the collar. Cut a piece of pink crepe three and one-half inches long and two and one-half inches wide; cut out a piece for the head to go through, forming a V in front, and beginning at the center of the waist, slope the collar a little towards the shoulders, giving the whole a pointed effect; edge this with stars, make a cap by drawing a piece of white crepe tightly about the head and gathering together in back. Trim with pink ribbon, and we have another maid, a typical little Gretchen.

"The dress of our No. 3 Doll forms a splendid setting to her dark beauty. The skirt, four inches long, is made on the same plan as the others, both upper and underskirt being of the same color, and a band of stars placed an inch from the bottom. The crepe is drawn loosely in front over a small padding of cotton and gummed down flat in back. A broad, plaited sash is placed about the waist and formed into a large bow at the back. A small ruffle, half an inch deep is glued to the upper edge of the waist, turned neatly over, and a band of stars glued on the ruffle around the neck. Two strips of crepe cut on the length, two inches in depth and two and one-half in length are used to form the sleeves. Gather each, separately, at the top and fasten to the arms. Pull out the lower edges and finish with a band of stars. Over these place a similar ruffle the same length, but only an inch in depth, and ornament in the same way. A strip of yellow crepe, an inch deep and three inches long, is gathered and glued to the head, bordered with stars and bent to suit the face. This, with a bow of ribbon standing on the top with long streamers forms the hat. Now, place three little stars carelessly on the belt, place the end of the ribbon coquettishly in her hands and she is all ready for her summer afternoon's walk.

"The costume for No. 3 Dancing Girl made on No. 3 jointed form, was fashioned as follows: The first skirt is double, cutting crepe four and one-quarter inches by one yard for each skirt; gather with thread and join around the waist in back. The second or over-skirt is single, being cut from crepe two and one-quarter inches by eighteen inches, which gather, join and place around the waist over the first skirt.

"Fit the bodice to form, padding but slightly, and cut pointed at the waist; line the sleeves and have merely a ruffle at arm hole. Narrow ribbon was tied around the shoulders and waist, finished with bows. A frill of crepe paper forms the hat which was also orna-mented with a small ribbon bow. With all edges of the dress tinted in water colors the effect is very much enhanced.

"No. 3 jointed form is also dressed as a Ballet Dancer in this wise: Make a double skirt of crepe paper about three-quarters of a yard wide and four inches long, fasten by sewing through the body and gluing the open ends together. For the waist, take a small piece of crepe about three inches square, draw it plainly in front over a slight padding to give the desired roundness and gather tightly about the waist. Cut the remainder of the crepe which hangs from the waist line into points, fashion the neck square, back and front, and finish with a band of gold stars. Bring your stars down around the waist—jacket like—gather two narrow strips of crepe about the arm scye and just touch the edge of the skirt and points of waist with gold paint to heighten the effect. Place two tiny ribbon bows upon the shoulders and with the arms curved above the head your danseuse is complete.

"Invaluable in this as in all crepe work is Dennison's Gum, which dries quickly and with-out stain. Price and description are given on page 14."

These dancing dolls ranged in size from nine and three-fourths inches, No. 3, to about fourteen inches, No. 5. No. 4 was eleven and one-half inches tall. They were eight, nine and ten cents apiece, according to size. The smallest doll in the catalog, six and one-half inches, sold for five cents!

Dennison's "Nursery Outfit" is described in the old catalog as follows: "We have made a complete outfit for paper doll making, which we call our "NURSERY OUTFIT." It includes one doll's dress, complete, a number of heads, also stiff paper bodies for new dresses, lace paper for edging and trimming, and an ample supply of TISSUE PAPER in selected colors for making dresses.

"It may be said of the paper dolls in this OUTFIT, with the TISSUE PAPER dresses, that they are far ahead of the old style of paper dolls in beauty and variety. Where the nursery is supplied with these the child's artistic instincts will be cultivated and its ingenuity stimulated. The softened, beautiful tints and colors of the tissue paper material are in themselves an education to the eye and the taste."

129.

130.

Jointed Form no 1   131

a

Jointed Form no. 2.

Corala   132

Dennison jointed dolls.

The outfit referred to above contained material for four complete dolls, six sheets of tissue, paper lace, star ornaments, silver embossed paper and a copy of a booklet of instructions, all for thirty-five cents.

Another article in Dennison's old catalog under the heading "Doll Dresses of Crepe and Tissue Paper" reads as follows: "The Dolls' heads and legs furnished by the Dennison Mfg. Co. in envelopes, together with dress and body forms and which are also part of Dennison's 'Nursery Outfit,' made up in Crepe or Tissue paper make quite a family of dolls. Various styles of boys' and girls' heads are also sold by most dealers in toys, fancy goods and stationery. The following directions describe the manner of making these dolls and a few of the elaborate costumes.

"A doll eleven inches high had the arms and legs cut in one with the body. The stockings are made of black tissue—No. 100—neatly gummed on the card-board. The shoes are of bronze paper, with gilt lines to mark the foxing and gilt dots for the buttons. An easel rest is gummed to the back of the body, near the shoulders.

"The head is an embossed picture; but before it is attached to the body, a fine plaiting of white tissue is gummed to the under side around the neck; the head is then attached in such a way that the top of the dress may be put under this plaiting; and each costume thus had the effect of a wide falling ruffle of white around the neck.

"The dress forms for a doll of this size should be cut of stiff white paper, and be seven inches long, five inches wide at the bottom, and two and one-quarter at the waist-line, which is a little less than two inches from the top. Do not forget to leave small tabs on each form, by which to hang the dress from the doll's shoulders. Each form should be covered with plain paper of the shade of which it is intended to make the dress.

"A dainty house-dress is of pale blue, in shade No. 36. Cut a plain piece of tissue eight by seven and one-half inches, and fold and gum a narrow hem and three tiny tucks near one end. Under the hem gum a fine plaiting which has been made of paper one inch wide. Shirr this dress along the top, and also along a line or two and one-half inches from the top, and gum these lines of shirring to the top edge and the waist-line respectively of the dress-form which had been previously prepared, forming a waist of the blouse or 'Fedora' style.

"Before the dress is attached to the form, however, the latter should have fine plaitings of white gummed in the arm scyes to answer for sleeves. At each side of the waist, a bunch of blue and white ribbons—strips of tissue one-fourth inch-wide should be placed.

"A much more elaborate costume is a 'Party Dress.' The foundation is prepared in the same way as for the dress just described. The shade of the sample dress was No. 81—pale pink—with white. A full ruching of pink and white borders the skirt and arm scyes. This is made of strips of the paper cut one inch wide, and finely plaited or shirred through the middle. The pink is then gummed to position, and the white placed inside of it and secured. After both are entirely dry, the ruching is carefully pulled into shape as a rose-plaiting. Long loops of pink and white paper ribbons are placed at each end of the waist-line.

"A street dress is of two shades, No. 120 and 68A; and the costume includes a hat. A full waist, not a blouse, is of white, with plaitings forming a 'V.' In these plaitings, each of which has two rows, the paper is so arranged that the darker shade is underneath, the lighter plaiting being finished with a heading. The skirt has a double ruching, as described for the party dress. A sash-belt of the lighter shade is finished at each end with a bunch of ribbons of the two shades, the loops and ends at the left hand of the doll being so long as to reach almost to the ruching.

"For the hat, cut a double strip of stiff paper one-half inch wide open at both top and bottom, and shaped to fit the top of the doll's head. Cut a strip of tissue of the lighter purple two inches wide, and crinkle finely cross-wise, leaving one edge plain. Gather the other edge very full on the fingers and gum to the top of the form, bringing both ends around and gumming them on the back of the form.

"Trim with loops of paper ribbon of both shades, and violets, both light and dark, and bring into Gainsborough shape by pulling up the brim here and there.

"Another dress has the neck cut square and finished with plaiting. This doll, of course, has no plaiting under the neck of the embossed picture which forms the head. Another has a guimp of white, shirred at the neck, with ruching forming a short, low waist. A sash has its ends at one side. Another has a full, short waist, with a plain tucked skirt, short sleeves, sash with wide ends—a charming model in white and blue for 'sweet simplicity.'

133.

No. 3 Jointed Form

134.

No. 3 Dancing Girl

135

a

b

Jointed dolls of Dennison Manufacturing Co. Two party
costumes for doll 135 are shown (a and b).

"Still another has the neck finished with lace paper. A boy's blouse has an open sailor collar edged with lace paper, the space at the neck filled in with white tucked paper. The sleeves are full and finished with lace-edged cuffs, and the knee-breeches are pasted flat on the form.

"A Little Lord Fauntleroy suit is of shade No. 100; it has collar and cuffs of lace paper, and a wide fringed sash.

"These are but every-day costumes compared with some which are made by cunning fingers. Skilled hands, guided by ingenious minds, have fashioned from paper the most elaborate imitations of the belles and beaux pictured amid the landscapes of Watteau. For these, embossed heads, having powdered and elaborately dressed hair, are chosen, and court-train and pannier, ruffled skirts and peach-blossom coats appear in all their glory. For these, however, the best directions are to be made by a careful study of a picture of some scene in which such figures are included, and we shall not attempt to describe the infinite variety that may be made."

Many of the articles in the old Dennison catalogs begin with a eulogy of the doll or its clothes. They make interesting reading. To quote:

"The great and undying popularity of paper dolls with children is well known to all who have anything to do with the care of the little ones. They are a source of endless pleasure and amusement to successive generations, and an invaluable aid to mother and nurse in supplying occupation for restless hands and eager minds in the nursery."

In another section of the catalog we have the following:

"So long as the world is peopled with children will dolls continue to hold sway over the childish heart; and so long as they continue to do so, so long will they have to be clothed. And their fashions must not be allowed to come to a standstill. 'A new dress' is the cry from the little ones, and that cry must be heard. In the paper line, as in every other, the dolls are always on the advance, and the paper doll of the child of today is as different from that of her great-grandmother years ago as black is from white. There is always something new on the market, and something which is sure to be pleasing."

The articles goes on to say that the jointed dolls are made in several sizes and various styles, from babies to ballet dancers, and can be had with or without dresses, and that there are thirty colors of crepe paper and a hundred and thirty-four shades of tissue from which to choose, not to mention gold star ornaments, paper lace, flitters, etc.

A great deal of ingenuity was shown in the making of these paper dresses, as evidenced by the number and variety which find their way into the hands of collectors. But long before Dennison's made easier this type of costume, little fingers were busy fashioning wardrobes from tissue and plaited paper with lace and flowers from old valentines. Some of these are exquisite, others crude, depending upon the ability and the age of the creator; all are interesting as the work and the love of children of another era. Mr. Wilbur Macey Stone in his booklet on paper dolls speaks feelingly of the old hand-made paper dolls and dresses, and tells of some of the vintage of 1860 to 1870 which came from the home of Charles Dudley Warner in Hartford. He says:

"They were all home-made dolls, and one, of about five inches tall, has the most elaborate costumes of any paper doll I ever saw. They are built up of plaited paper and overlays of great ingenuity, while the evening gown, with a train, is made of blue tissue paper with an underskirt of white chiffon and lace. The skirt is garnished with white embossed flowers from an old valentine. While all of these dresses are fronts only, they surely come pretty near to being three-dimensional creations. They would serve as excellent models for a dress-maker."

The doll illustrated as "Mary" (No. 136) differs from the other activated dolls shown in that only the arms move and the dress is printed. Colors are white with pink ribbon trimming and slipper bows. Stockings are red with black slippers. The doll is a ten and one-half inch brunette and belongs to Mrs. Mallon.

"Mary," arms only activated, at right above. Activated
doll at left has printed blouse, but skirt of real material.

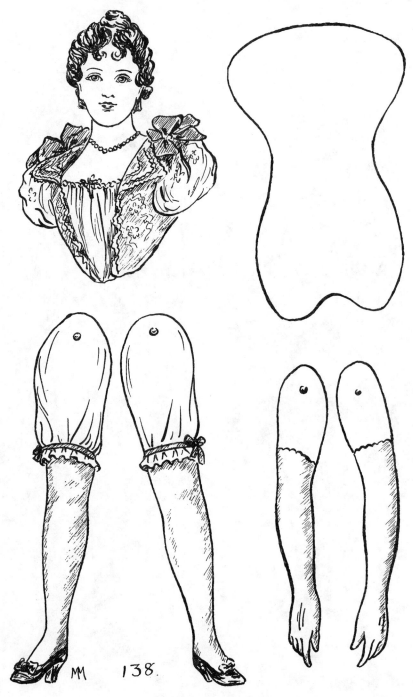

MM   138.

Unassembled Lady Doll.

The doll at left of "Mary" (No. 137) is in the same style except that the blouse and leg wear only are printed. The skirt and lace underwear showing is of real material.

The unassembled "lady" doll (No. 138) also has the bodice printed as well as leg and arm wear. She is a brunette and wears a white bodice with yellow sleeveless Eton jacket with yellow bows on the shoulders. She has pale blue gloves, shoes and slippers with matching ribbons in the pant-legs.

"Edith" (No. 139) is an especially attractive nine and one-half inch activated paper doll with a skirt and apron of material added underneath the printed waist.

The baby doll (No. 140) at right of "Edith" is referred to in Dennison's catalog. It is nine inches tall.

"Corala," Mrs. Lake's six and one-half inch doll, "Jointed Form No. 2," and "Jointed Form No. 1," also are referred to in the catalog. The dressed doll under the arm of "Corala" shows how she should be dressed. It was taken from the Dennison catalog.

**Activated child doll (139) with skirt and apron of real material
added. At right, Dennison's activated baby doll, jointed Form No. 8.**

The six attached heads are the ones referred to in the above mentioned catalog as those that may be purchased at stationery supplies shops. Dennison's supplied the body parts.

The well-known English firm, Raphael Tuck & Sons Co., Ltd., also published activated paper dolls. Those illustrated are undated, but the notation on the back of the doll "Publishers to Their Majesties, The King and Queen" places them about the date 1894; many of the Tuck dolls of this period bore the same notation. On the reverse side of each figure is a verse by Clifton Bingham appropriate to the doll. Each carries a toy or what-have-you in either hand, which swings out of sight at the back of the doll. Only the arms move.

"Daisy Dimple" (No. 141) has yellow hair and blue eyes. She wears a green dress and hat, the latter trimmed with one pink and one red rose and white feathers. A red ribbon about the waist matches in shade the slippers, and the lace at neck. Green lace forms the ruffle of the skirt. The white boy doll carried by "Daisy Dimple" is dressed in blue and red, the darky doll in yellow and red. The following is printed on the back of the figure:

"Dolly Daisy Dimple. Puzzled.

"I'm Daisy Dimple, if you please,
"Have you two dollies sweet as these?
"If so, why are they, as you see,
"One black as ink, one white like me!"

The suit of the clown doll (No. 142) is half red and half blue with white figures in the material. The ruffle at neck and pompons down the center of the

141   142

Daisy Dimple   Clown

Raphael Tuck's "Daisy Dimple" and clown dolls.

143

Chinee

144   145

Pierrot   Swiss

Raphael Tuck dolls; hinged at the shoulders, and activated by a cord at the back of the figure.

costume and on the green cap are yellow, matching the cymbals. The shoes are black; one with a blue pompon, one with a red pompon. Printing on the reverse side of the doll reads:

"Clown Doll. A Figure of Fun.

"I am a merry little clown,
"I never grumble, sigh or frown,
"It's better far to laugh than cry
"Whatever happens, so say I."

Oddly enough, the paper doll in the Japanese costume (No. 143) is labelled "Dolly from Chinaland. A Happy Chinee." The verse reads:

"Please, I have come from Chinaland,
"With flowers and fan in either hand;
"I'm happy now—if you like me,
"Then I shall doubly happy be."

The costume has a red background with figures in blue, green and purple. There are purple bands at the bottom and sleeves of the kimono. In one hand is a blue fan decorated with white birds; in the other, yellow chrysanthemums.

Pierrot (No. 144) has brown eyes and reddish yellow hair. He wears a blue and white checked suit with red pompons and a white ruffle around his neck. A tan cap matches his shoes, the former trimmed with red pompons. The girl doll in one hand of the figure is a blonde dressed in red with green pompons. Punch, on the other hand, has a white ruffle at his neck and green streamers with yellow pompons. His hat is yellow with a green brim trimmed at the points with red balls. The following is printed on the back of the figure:

"Pierrot Doll. Four Smiles.

"We're Judy, Punch and little me,
"A smiling three, as you'll agree;
"And when you see us, there'll be four,
"You're sure to smile and make one more."

The Swiss doll (No. 145) has blue eyes and dark hair. She wears a green jumper dress over a white blouse, a blue and white checked apron, green shoes with yellow buckles, red cap and stockings. A white lamb in one hand has a blue neck ribbon and the base is green with yellow trim. The toy cow is yellow with brown markings and wears a red ribbon with a yellow bell. The base has the same coloring as that of the lamb. Printing on the back of the figure reads:

"Swiss Dolly. Friends from the Farm.

"I've just come from an Alpine Farm.
"A pet from there upon each arm.
"I would have brought them all to you,
"But could not carry more than two."

All these dolls are hinged at the shoulders and activated by a cord from the back of the figure. In order to keep the arms extended one pulls down the cord and fixes it into the slit at the foot of the model. When in first position, the arms are at the back of the doll.

The dolls are reproduced through the courtesy of Miss Howard.

The Pantin of Punch (No. 146) illustrated in its unassembled form, is one of a series printed in Germany about 1924. Colors are red, orange and black. It is operated in the usual manner by cords attached to the limbs at the back of the doll.

146

Unassembled Pantin of Punch, from Germany, circa 1924.

Chapter XIII

Novelties

THE United States Patent Office sounds like a dull place to visit, but when one thinks of the records of hopes and ambitions it has held throughout the years as he pores through the patent files of any particular subject in which the searcher is interested, it becomes more than a place of mere statistics. In these files are many papers pertaining to novelty paper dolls, some of which were marketed, others probably not.

As stated before, it is interesting to note that in many cases, years after the patent was granted, the same principle was presented to the public as a new idea. "Round-about dolls," already referred to, were advertised by a prominent concern in 1938-1939 as a "new and constructive idea." The "new and constructive idea" was patented June 22, 1897—see No. 147 patent paper No. 585092—by Edward Tinkham Gibson of Minneapolis, Minnesota—four decades earlier. There were some differences between the "round-about" of 1897 and that of 1938, but the principle involved was the same. With reference to the Gibson paper doll, the round-about skirt was part of the doll itself. In the later doll, a "round-about" dress fitted over a flat figure.

A paper doll which sat in a separate chair (No. 148) was patented by Anna F. Fisher of Hempstead, N. Y., on February 22, 1921. About twenty-seven years earlier a doll which sat in a separate chair (No. 149) was published by McLaughlin's Coffee Company to advertise their product. In the two cases, the method of seating was different, but the idea was the same. A study of the sketches will show the difference. The two large tabs, one on either side of the McLaughlin doll, fit into the chair, which is cut at dotted line. The doll sketched on the patent paper numbered 1,369,093 demonstrates clearly the method Miss Fisher used for manipulating her doll.

The Lion Coffee blacksmith "Outfit 10," (No. 150), contributed by Miss Howard, consists of an anvil with fire, the blacksmith, and two customers, only one of the latter shown in the sketch. The blacksmith is a boy with blue and white striped shirt, tan apron and black shoes and stockings. He fits into a slot over the anvil. The young customer wears a blue dress with white apron, red cap and black stockings and high buttoned shoes. Both figures have light brown hair. The eyes of the girl are blue; those of the boy, brown. The dolls and anvil outfit are made to stand by bending back the standards. The girl not in the sketch is the same as that shown except that the eyes are brown and the hair darker, and an extra coat comes with her. The date is close to 1900.

Another novelty contributed by Miss Howard are the attached triplet baby girls (No. 151) advertising James Pyle's Pearline, "the original washing compound." The dolls' dresses are white and the sashes,—reading from left to right,—blue, pink and green with ribbons in caps to match. On the dress of the

(No Model.) 2 Sheets—Sheet 1.

E. T. GIBSON.
PAPER TOY.

No. 585,092.

Patented June 22, 1897.

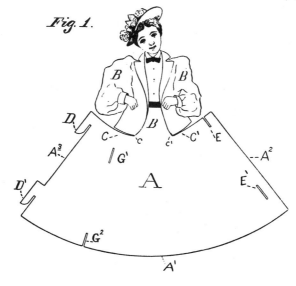

Fig. 1.

Fig. 2.

Witnesses
C. F. Kilgore
B. B. Meloon

Inventor.
Edward T. Gibson
By his Attorney
Edward T. Gibson

147.

Patent for the E. T. Gibson Paper "Round-about" dolls.

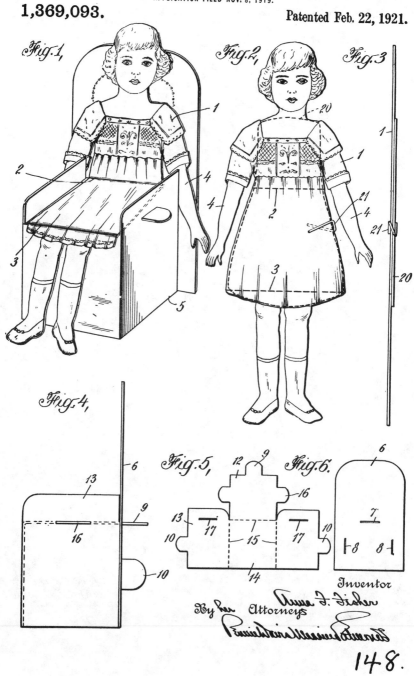

A. F. FISHER.
TOY.
APPLICATION FILED NOV. 8, 1919.

1,369,093.

Patented Feb. 22, 1921.

Fig.1,   *Fig.2,*   *Fig.3*

Fig.4,

Fig.5,   *Fig.6.*

Inventor
Anna F. Fisher
By her   Attorneys

148.

Patent for Anna Fisher's doll which sat in a separate chair.

149.

Doll and chair published by McLaughlin's Coffee Co., circa 1894.

central figure is printed "Our Mammas use Pearline." The reverse side of the figures is filled with advertising, including the phrase: "The birth of Pearline was the beginning of better things." Directions for making the three-fold doll stand were "This will stand alone if folded like a screen."

J. and P. Coats' dolls made to advertise spool cotton, about 1895, included an interesting novelty doll with three revolving heads, each with a different expression. Since they were printed both back and front, the figure (No. 152) really represented six dolls in one. A study of the sketches will show how the doll was operated. On one side the heads were brunettes, on the other side, blondes. The dress attached to the doll is yellow with purple jacket, and cuffs with white bands; purple sash and trimming at bottom; black shoes and stockings. The reverse side shows a different costume. The hat with the single plume goes with the yellow dress. It is purple to match the jacket, trimming around brim the same shade as the dress. Flowers at the base of the plume are blue. The reverse of the hat matches in color the upper part of the separate dress, or the upside down part shown in the sketch. The latter is red-brown with blue trimmings, and has light blue sleeves. The side in natural position is purple with yellow bows and ribbon bands, pink sleeves and white lace revers. The remaining hat matches. This doll, and the Coachman and Brougham Set 2, No. 153, were also contributed by Miss Howard.

Outfit no. 10

Lion Coffee blacksmith and his customer.

Triplet baby girls which advertised James Pyle's Pearline, "the original washing compound."

152.

J. & P. Coats dolls, used to advertise spool cotton about 1895. These included an interesting
novelty doll with three revolving heads, each having a different facial expression. They
were printed both back and front and really represented six dolls in one. Detached
revolving heads (a); separate costumes (b); hats (c and d).

The coach-brougham set consists of a chestnut colored horse with white saddle, a black brougham trimmed with yellow stripes and a red seat over which are thrown blue blankets; a lady with red blouse trimmed in yellow, black fur at edges of collar and muff, hat to match, and a green skirt; a gentleman with blue coat and black high-topped hat; and a coachman in tan costume and black shoes. The brougham is attached to the horse by placing the shaft through slots on either side of the saddle, and the three figures are placed in appropriate positions through a slot which runs almost all the way across the top part of the brougham. This set appeared in the 1890's.

Some of the paper dolls patented were used in a slightly different form by the publishers. Thus we have a very similar idea to the William T. Jefferson paper doll, No. 154, patented March 12, 1895, patent No. 535,621, used by the Barbour Brothers Company, Dougherty's New England Condensed Meat Co., Clark's O. N. T. Spool Cotton and others who advertised their ware by means of the paper doll. These are described in the chapter on advertising dolls.

The coachman and brougham set of McLaughlin Coffee.

(No Model.)

W. T. JEFFERSON.
PAPER DOLL.

No. 535,621. Patented Mar. 12, 1895.

WITNESSES:
Gustav Dieterich.
John H. Ehlenbeck.

INVENTOR
William T. Jefferson,
BY
Chas. C. Gill
ATTORNEY.

154.

William T. Jefferson paper doll patent of 1895.

156

155.

a

**Santa Claus doll; swinging arm with coin and purse (a);
upper left, doll dressed in real materials.**

157   *158*   *159*

The two dolls at left and center were made to represent flowers, and were quite common in the late nineteenth century. The two-faced baby doll at the right is made up from the sheets of busts referred to in the chapter on activated dolls.

Mrs. Mallon has a novel paper Santa Claus doll with one swinging arm; money is held in one hand which swings into a purse held in the other hand. Santa stands by bending back the flap at dotted line, as shown in the illustration No. 155.

The little doll at the left of Santa, No. 156, also belongs to Mrs. Mallon. It is made from one of the many printed figures on the market in the 1890's. The doll is attractively dressed with real materials.

Paper dolls made to represent flowers were quite common in the late nineteenth century. The two illustrated, Nos. 157 and 158, are from Dennison's catalog of 1894.

The two-faced paper baby is made up from one of the sheets of busts referred to in the chapter on activated dolls. Skirt and legs are crudely hand-made, but a great deal of care was exercised in making a three-dimensional bottle of hardened cotton batting. It was placed in the hand by cutting the latter around the edge. The doll is owned by Mrs. Douse.

In December, 1938, the magazine *Antiques* pictured a so-called fortune-telling doll whose billowing petticoats were composed of individual sheets of paper, each bearing a printed prophecy.

From the little Sixth Avenue, New York, shop referred to in another chapter came the beautifully lithographed sheet of paper doll cutouts (No. 160) fastened together by tiny tabs illustrated here in black and white. Dolls like these embellished many a cardboard village scene and many a home-made valentine in the last century.

The Royal Canadian Mounted Police with their colorful red jackets and blue trousers, and noble, high-stepping steeds always have been full of interest to young and old alike. The three cut-outs illustrated, (161, 162, 163), were taken from a sheet of eleven such owned by Mrs. Lake. Reading from left to right, the horses are colored, respectively, white, gray and tan. The "mounties" are in regulation uniform. These were purchased in Mexico City and instructions for mounting are given in Spanish.

In this country "Teddy" Roosevelt and his Rough Riders and paper soldiers of the Spanish-American war delighted both boys and girls about the turn of the century, thanks to McLoughlin Brothers.

Mr. Stone tells in his booklet about the thousands of paper soldiers he had in the early seventies of the last century, "each mounted on a little block of wood so as to stand bravely against the enemy's guns. Our cannon," says Mr. Stone, "were of wood, the motive force rubber bands, and the ammunition dried peas." Some years earlier, England, and no doubt other European countries, printed embossed, die-cut soldiers in brilliant hues. The same has been done for many generations and grown men of today remember these childhood treasures. The writer will not forget how excited her husband was when he found in a little shop in Germany in 1935 sheets of brightly colored and embossed soldiers, the same as he had played with in America when he was a boy.

Among the novelty paper dolls might be included the cutout doll forms with a separate head to fit into the neck of any one of the forms which came with toy-books in the early part of the nineteenth century, referred to in an earlier chapter. Miss Howard reports finding recently "a small book, Lauretta of the Temple of Fancy series, c. 1830. Hand-written in brown ink; f's for s's; illustrations all headless, with one head for all, this attached to a string so reader may swing it to any illustration, slipping the tab into a slot on back of the illustration." The original of Miss Howard's book was published in England; hers is evidently a copy. This was often done by the skillful in early days when not everyone could afford to buy books.

Between 1810 and 1825 America brought out these toy-books, but since they did not at that time have the facilities for die-cutting the dolls, they issued them in sheets bound into the book, rather than inserting cutouts in a pocket at the back of the book, European fashion. After 1840, however, completely American versions of the English paper doll toy-books were made. Crosby, Nichols & Co. of Boston employed another publisher of paper dolls, John Green Chandler (see chapter on early dolls) to design paper dolls for the books "Jack and His Pony," "Betty the Milkmaid," "Fanny Gray," etc. It often happened that outdoor and indoor scenes were part of the footrest of the doll, so that the doll complete was shown feeding chickens or petting a lamb, or occupied indoors.

In America it is difficult to find old picture books made from cutouts by eighteenth and early nineteenth century children. Europe is much more fortunate in the possession of this sort of thing than we are. Two of these picture books dating about 1800 may be seen in Munich at the Bavarian National Museum. They show a complete house of a wealthy Nuremberg citizen of the period; members of the household, their clothing, furniture, utensils, pictures,

Lithographed sheet of paper doll cut-outs from Germany,
bought at Burton's, Sixth Avenue, New York.

Three cut-outs, taken from a sheet of eleven owned by Mrs. Lake, and purchased in
Mexico City. The Royal Canadian "mounties" are in regulation uniform.

164

**Paper cut-out in the Munich Museum showing picture gallery
of about 1830, attended by patrons.**

etc. Cupboards open to reveal their treasures. Outdoor scenes also are por-
trayed. ,There are children at play in the garden, street scenes, the sledging
party, the hunt; in fact, everything connected with the life of a rich citizen.

Among other interesting paper cut-outs in the Munich Museum is a picture
gallery of about 1830, nine and one-half inches high, made of colored cardboard
and attended by patrons. (See illustration No. 164.) Other cutouts in the
Museum are a counting house, a market place, a drawing room and a nursery.

At the Landesgewerbe Museum in Stuttgart is a toy church made about
1840 by M. Trentsensky. It is lithographed in color and consists of eighty-six
pieces, the former property of Emperor Franz Joseph of Austria.

In the same museum one may also see the fore-runner of our modern "pop-
up" books—the 1840 "Surprise Picture Book" referred to in the second chapter
of this book.

Illustration No. 165 "Paper Dolls at a Fancy Dress Party, 1807," is from
the old toy catalog of G. H. Bestelmeier of Nuremberg.

Wax was sometimes used in decorating a cardboard house. An example of
this may be seen in the rococo "Salon" from a German doll house of 1740 at the
Maxmilian Museum in Augsburg.

An interesting Viennese paper theatre of about 1840 is in the Volkskunst
Museum, Dresden.

165

Paper dolls at a fancy dress party, 1807, from the old toy
catalog of G. H. Bestelmeier, Nuremberg.

Other European countries also brought out fine paper toys. One of the most beautiful and interesting cardboard theatres the writer has ever seen came from Barcelona, Spain. The twenty-five by sixteen-inch theatre is complete in every detail. The pillared arch shows behind it three sets of curtains—the main curtain pulls up—and across the top is a beautifully modelled papier mâché frieze. Notched wings which open up are made to accommodate six pieces which combine, section by section, to make the first scene in Act I of "Violeta" and eight pieces for the second act of the play. They are so arranged that different colors of isinglass show through arches, windows and larger openings, making possible a lighting effect of real beauty.

England has for many generations enjoyed quite a reputation for paper dolls and cut-outs. Pollock's paper pantomime characters are described in A. E. Wilson's *Penny Plain, Twopence Colored.* Here are paper theatre characters galore, portraits of many nineteenth century actors which otherwise might have been lost, for while the toy theatre was Pollock's principal business, many of the characters from the stage of grown-ups were represented, besides contemporary celebrities such as the young Queen Victoria and Prince Albert, Queen Adelaide, Napoleon, Wellington, etc. Among the favorite actresses pictured were Mrs. Faucet as the Queen of Denmark, Fanny Kemble as Juliet and Madam Vestris as Dewdrop. The prints were hand-colored, as were many paper dolls of the period.

American women of today have pleasant childhood memories of imported English cardboard theatres, as well as theatre sets made in our own country. The simple eight by twelve-inch Play-Sho of *Red Riding Hood, Snow White*— not the recent movie version—and others produced by the Buzza Co., Minneapolis, Minnesota, are interesting.

Cardboard manger sets, houses, castles, stores, markets, etc., displayed in the five-and-ten-cent stores have found eager customers. Books of cutouts in modern times are attractive and instructive. Not all of us can see the famous Coleen Moore Dolls' Castle, but many have enjoyed it in paper form.

Through Milton Bradley's cutouts, American children have enjoyed foreign and domestic villages and scenes from the history of our country, have learned authentic stories of big industries, the delights of poster-making with cutouts, etc.

The habitat of paper dolls follows as closely as possible the habitat of the real doll, but on paper it can be made elaborate at low cost. Even before the advent of machine-made paper in 1798 German engravers brought out a series of pictures meant only for cutting out and have continued to do so until modern times. Gorgeous real doll houses and furnishings properly scaled to size were luxuries that only the wealthy could enjoy, but with the advent of large-scale paper toy manufacture in the eighteenth and especially in the nineteenth century, when machine-made paper was available in large quantities at low cost, almost any child could enjoy these miniatures in paper form.

There are in this country in the hands of collectors some very beautiful and elaborate cardboard dolls' houses, some with furniture that fits into the walls and cribs with slots through the tops of the blankets to put the babies in and many other devices to make a realistic set-up. Many of the elaborate ones came from Europe. The earliest dolls' house to be patented in America seems to be Patent No. 79,782 by Emily S. Russell of Plymouth, Massachusetts, in the year 1868. It is the plain little house reproduced here. (Illustration No. 166).

In the possession of the writer is a most practical and interesting dolls' house of cardboard patented by McLoughlin Brothers in 1894. It consists of four rooms, kitchen, dining room, parlor and bedroom, each twelve inches square, arranged in such a manner that it can fold up like a book. The flooring of the kitchen is in imitation tile; carpet and rugs printed realistically decorate the floors of the other rooms. Doors, mantelpieces, pictures, etc., are printed on the walls, and there is an open archway between the dining room and parlor for the paper inhabitants to pass through. The dolls' house presents a good picture of average middle-class house furnishings in the 1890's.

Among the most interesting of all the cutouts in the eighteenth and nineteenth centuries was the peepshow with cardboard figures. Those who think they do not know what a peepshow is will remember the fancy besugared Easter egg hollowed out to show a scene inside, much in evidence at Easter time years ago and still being sold in season. The idea of the old peepshow is the same but on a much larger and more elaborate scale. A good example of an eighteenth century peepshow with Freemason's lodge may be seen at the Landesgewerbe Museum in Stuttgart, although it is only three and three-fourths inches in height. An 1874 traveling peepshow is sketched in a little book called *Sights At a Peepshow*, by Mrs. George Cupples, printed by T. Nelson & Sons, Paternoster Row, Edinburgh; and New York. The peepshow with children looking in, and one of the pictures showing a domestic scene are reproduced here. (See illustration No. 167.)

The first model for the peepshow was of a religious nature, the ever-popular Christmas Crib. Just as early masters of painting confined their subjects to religious themes, the legitimate theatre, the marionette theatre, and finally the paper theatre, brought to the fore the teachings of religion. But not for long.

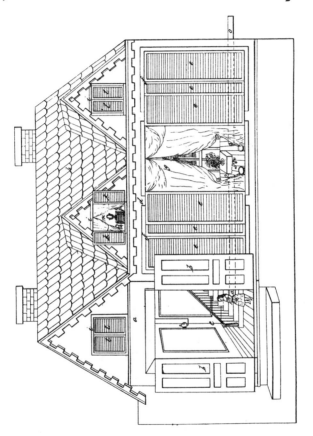

E. S. Russell,

Toy House,

№ 79,782,   Patented July 7, 1868.

Witnesses: Inventor:
M. W. Frothingham.   Emily S. Russell
J. B. Hill.   by her attys.
                                              Crosby Halsted & Gould

166

Cardboard Toy House patented by Emily S. Russell, of Plymouth.

United States Patent Office.

EMILY S. RUSSELL, OF PLYMOUTH, MASSACHUSETTS.

Letters Patent No. 79,782, dated July 7, 1868.

TOY-HOUSE.

The Schedule referred to in these Letters Patent and making part of the same.

TO ALL WHOM IT MAY CONCERN:

Be it known that I, EMILY S. RUSSELL, of Plymouth, in the county of Plymouth, and State of Massachusetts, have invented an Improved Toy-House; and I do hereby declare that the following, taken in connection with the drawings which accompany and form part of this specification, is a description of my invention sufficient to enable those skilled in the art to practise it.

The invention relates to the construction of a toy designed particularly for the use of little girls in playing house with dolls, and consists primarily in a toy-house, or a representation of a house, made of pasteboard or equivalent thin material, having swinging doors and blinds, each of which, when open, shows, in the back ground, a representation of a hall, drawing-room, chamber, or other apartment, while, when closed, it has the natural appearance of doors or windows closed by ordinary doors or blinds.

The invention also consists in making such a toy of two sheets, placed together, and united at opposite edges, the doors and windows being made in the outer sheet, (which represents the outside of the house,) and the pictures of the rooms being painted or printed upon the inner sheet, opposite the doors and windows, this construction allowing paper dolls to be slipped in between the sheets, and to be thus moved from room to room within the house.

The invention also consists in combining with such a house a paper doll or dolls, with means for moving such a doll from room to room without directly touching it.

The drawing represents a front elevation of such a toy, showing one end, the side, and the roof of a house in perspective.

a denotes the end of the house, having doors, *b b*, opening into the hall *c*.

d denotes the side of the house, with sets of blinds, *e e*, each set closing over a window, as seen at *f*, or opening, and disclosing the apartment back of the window, as seen at *g*.

In the roof *h* are windows, as seen at *i*, each having blinds to open and close, as seen, respectively, at *k* and *l*, the open blinds *k* showing a chamber, *m*, with the furniture therein, while the open blinds *e* show a boudoir, and the open doors *b* disclose the hall and hall-stairs.

Each set of closed blinds covers a similar representation of an apartment, each apartment being differently furnished from the others, so that the whole appearance is readily changed by opening and closing different windows.

It will thus be seen that by having several door and window-openings, thus capable of being opened or closed, a great variety of changes can be produced, greatly to the amusement of a child.

When the house is made of two sheets, the door and blinds are preferably made by cutting the card or sheet for the top, bottom, and outer edge of each, and then folding back the piece thus partially cut out, the fold constituting the hinge. If made of one card, each blind or door may have a border sufficiently wide to admit of its being cemented to the front.

The outside of the card, and the outer surface of each door or blind, is colored or printed to give it the desired appearance, (and the surroundings of the house may be shown in imitation of shrubbery, vines, &c.,) and the space back of each window or door-opening is also colored or printed to properly represent the apartment beyond, the construction I prefer having the blinds, doors, and outside of the house represented on one sheet, and the apartments on the sheet placed upon the back of this. When thus made, a doll, *n*, may be slid between the sheets, and, by means of a wire or a strip of card, *o*, attached to it, may be made to move from room to room, as will be readily understood.

It will be obvious that a toy thus made will conduce to the quiet amusement of children old enough to play with dolls, and especially to the diversion of little girls playing together, having great attractions for many children over any toy-houses and furniture requiring building or setting up.

There is nothing about the toy liable to break or to get under foot, and it shows, or may be made to show, a great variety of furniture and inside decorations.

I claim a toy-house, made of two thin sheets of material secured together, the outer sheet having swinging doors and blinds, concealing or disclosing representations of apartments on the inner sheet, and the space between the sheets being adapted to movements of a doll, *n*, substantially as described.

EMILY S. RUSSELL.

Witnesses:
JNO. J. RUSSELL,
J. WALTER SPOONER.

Patent for the Toy House, shown on the preceding page.

167

167-2

**Peepshow with children looking in; and to the right, one
of the scenes they would see, showing home life; 1874.**

People soon became more interested in the busy life of the times, things that
were close at hand, for they could understand them better, and so the peepshow
became devoted to purely secular subjects. The house of the peepshow was usually
a wooden box lighted from above, and looked at through a lens set in the front,
which magnified and gave to the figure a three-dimensional effect. Inside was a
picture cut out in several planes and placed, one behind another in proper perspective. Some of the eighteenth century peepshows were gorgeous, and the
range of subjects almost as great as the motion picture of today. Boys and girls
of that period probably enjoyed them just as much as modern children delight in
the movies. No fair or festival was considered complete without a good peepshow. It would be an interesting project to build up a peepshow based on
eighteenth century scenes, and one showing the modern scene. What an at-
traction at a public exhibition of paper dolls and paper figures!

In the early years of the twentieth century novelty sets of paper dolls
especially designed for the Christmas trade appeared. One folder containing
the doll and outfit is in the shape of Santa Claus wearing a blue coat, another in
a red coat, and a third folder is in the shape of a Christmas tree. Both Santa and
the Christmas tree are folded at the base, and on the inside cover are pockets
fitted out with a paper doll child, clothes and toys, all beautifully colored and
embossed. The Christmas tree is lighted by candles, as was the custom when the
set was printed. Two sets—covers and contents—are printed here. (See
illustrations No. 168 and 169.) It seems odd that so many things can be stored
away in the pockets of one small cover. Santa and the Christmas tree are each
five and three-quarters inches tall, and the doll is four inches high. The
embossing is similar to work of this kind done at about the turn of the century.

168

Cover design of early 20th century Santa Claus, in which was
enclosed doll, clothes, toys, such as shown on the opposite page.

Coming nearer to our own time, Tana Graitser in 1934 designed some attractive paper dolls twenty to twenty-four inches tall, to advertise dress materials.
These were sponsored by a manufacturer of silk to show off the latest materials
he supplied from time to time.

Most of us are familiar with modern novelty paper dolls, the closing-eye
dolls found in the five-and-ten-cent stores a short time ago; ones with natural
hair pasted on; others with ruffles of real silk or rayon or lace sewn onto the
skirt and sometimes the waist also; and the "magic" paper dolls covered with
magnetized felt, so that clothes simply placed on the dolls adhere satisfactorily.
The number of novelty dolls is legion.

Collectors are acquiring the best of our modern paper dolls, among the most
interesting of which are portrait dolls of prominent persons, those which show
the best styles of our time, and those which tell a story. In 1940 Betty Camp-

168-2.

Contents of the Santa Claus folder shown on opposite page.

bell made a most attractive set of dolls to represent an eighteenth century family of old Williamsburg, Virginia, the city recently restored. A story by Mary Selby accompanied the dolls, which were published by Samuel Gabriel Sons & Co. of New York, who also published another charming set by the same artist with a story by Susan S. Popper. The latter set includes the famous *Pinky* and *The Blue Boy,* easily recognizable.

Another interesting paper doll book, published by Howell, Soskin, Inc., is *The Martha Washington Doll Book* by Aline Bernstein.

The Royal Ontario Museum of Archaeology publishes an uncolored but educational doll called "Roma" with costumes from 1815 to 1892.

There are not as many amateur artists today painting paper dolls as there were in earlier years, which is a pity, for dolls lovingly and skillfully painted by hand whether in 1800 or 1951 will always be treasured by the connoisseur. "A thing of beauty is a joy forever."

Paper dolls for the trade, which anyone may acquire, come and go so quickly that it is well to keep an eye on present publications. Collectors who missed the opportunity to buy in paper from the Dionne Quintuplets and the little English princesses are most regretful. It would be infeasible to buy all the paper dolls which flood the market, but those that have special merit should not be allowed to pass into the limbo of forgotten things. Future collectors and students of costume design will value our well-selected dolls as much as we prize those of years gone by.

The doll and other playthings found in the folder
of Christmas tree, shown on opposite page.

**Christmas tree cover design which, like the Santa
Claus shown on page 174, contained doll, clothes,
and toys.**

Chapter XIV

Polish Paper Dolls

URIOUS things happen after a great war—big events and little ones—but often the small things are significant. It was an act of friendship, of international good will, a wish to reciprocate kindness done that brought about the receipt from Poland by a member of the Dollology Club of Washington, D. C., Mrs. Beatrice McKenna, of a set of old paper dolls in native peasant costume.

American artists have issued through their publishers sets of paper dolls in foreign dress from time to time, basing their sketches on illustrations from "The National Geographic" and other magazines dealing with travel abroad. It is seldom, however, that we find a set of original foreign paper dolls with native peasant outfits not made for export. The five and one-half-inch dolls illustrated were sent to Mrs. McKenna as a gesture of appreciation for clothing sent a young woman in Poland whose family, like thousands of others in war-devastated countries, finds it difficult to obtain enough clothing material to supply minimum needs.

It has not been easy to decipher the Polish names of the paper dolls from the unfamiliar foreign hand-writing, but as far as possible, the following are accurate.

No. 170 is the blond young man Kasiubski. He wears a white shirt with red bow tie, pants with stripes in two shades of medium blue, and black boots. The extra vest *a*, is dark blue with red buttons, over a white shirt with red tie, The coat, *b*, also is of dark blue with red lining, collar and cuffs, red buttons and red and green scarf tied around the waist. His plum colored hat has a blue band.

No. 171 is unnamed, but for convenience we shall call her Lucy. She has blue eyes and light brown hair. Her white blouse and cerulean blue vest, the latter edged in deep orange, are embroidered in pink to match her plain pink apron, which almost covers her green skirt with its orange bands. Gray shoes, and necklace of double-stranded pink beads complete the costume.

The sketch at right of the doll *a*, fits over the latter by means of tabs indicated.

The vest is deep pink with lighter pink flowers, interspersed with small designs in blue and green. A plain white apron almost covers the skirt—the latter matching the vest—except that it is banded with plain deep pink. The main design in the shawl is black, high-lighted with pink, blue and green. A white blouse is embroidered in purple, and the white, lace-edged headgear is trimmed with roses. Pink beads adorn the neck.

The remaining costume is in two parts. The design in the otherwise white vest *b*, is mainly pink, high-lighted with yellow and light blue, the banding of deeper blue; kerchief matches. The blouse is white with designs in deep plum color. The apron, *c*, to go with this vested blouse is striped in salmon pink with contrasting stripes of blue and gray. A blue skirt edged with red is evident underneath the apron. Shoes are deep plum with orange trimming; necklace pink; stockings white.

Kasiubski 170

**Polish paper doll, a young man named Kasiubski,
with his shirt and vest (a), and coat (b).**

Lucy

171.

a.

b.

c.

Lucy, another of the "good will" dolls from Poland.

Lusyckie, who wears the striped costume of the Province Lowicz; her blouse with vest (a); skirt (b); jacket with headgear (c); headgear (d); shawl (e); headpiece (f); small headgear (g).

Written on the back of doll No. 172 is the name *Lusyckie*. She wears the striped costume of the province or parish of Lowicz. The widest stripes are of black and orange, with orange the predominant color of the vest. Black or dark plum color is the predominant color of the skirt. Narrower stripes are yellow, green, blue, deep pink and orange. The apron is rather a deep shade of blue with deep pink edging on the pocket. The blouse is white with trimming to match the lighter shades of the costume.

The separate costume, in two parts, is striped in the same manner except that the coloring is different. Widest stripes in the vest are green edged with red, the next widest black edged with red. The blouse *a*, is similar to the blouse on the doll itself, except that the sleeves are long with embroidered cuffs. The double-flounced apron covering the wide separate skirt, *b*, has wide stripes of green edged with pink, orange and black. The widest stripes of the skirt itself are orange edged with blue, green, pink and red. Shoes are black. The separate jacket, *c*, is purplish red with white fur. Trimming around edge is pink. But-tons match the jacket. Orange beads add a further touch of color. The head-piece is green with pink flowers and pink edging. Bridal headgear, *a*, just underneath the jacket is of every hue.

The shawl, *e*, at upper right is white with plum colored embroidered flowers and edging over a white blouse. The extra headgear underneath, *f*, is of white figured material over a crown of flowers and pleated ribbon with flowered streamers. The tiny headpiéce, *g*, underneath this is of blue with pink flowers.

Knekowanki, with typical Polish blue eyes and blonde hair. Sack (a); skirt (b); shawl with cap (c); large shawl (d); small shawl (e); bouquet (f); coat (g).

Knekowanki is the name given doll No. 173. She has the typical blue eyes and yellow hair of her native land. Her apron has narrow stripes in orange, green and blue, matching the coloring of the overblouse. Not much is seen of the pink skirt under the wide apron. The bottom of the skirt, visible at the left of the doll, has contrasting bands of green and yellow edged with white rickrack braid. The usual white blouse is trimmed with pink, and beads match the trimming. Her coat, g, at left of the doll, is blue with pink embroidery and tassels. A white embroidered skirt shows underneath. Shoes are blue with pink lacings.

The two-piece ensemble at the extreme left consists of a figured pink jacket, a, with white embroidery at the neck and sleeves, the jacket edged with a narrow band of blue. The apron b, is all white, embroidered, and the skirt showing underneath is white figured in orange and green. It is trimmed with bands of orange and green rickrack braid.

The separate head and shoulder piece holding book, c, shows a white scarf and headpiece embroidered in pink. The tiny cap at right is variegated in shades of purple, blue and orange, with red feather trimming.

The large shawl, d, is light green with pink flowers and dark green foliage, and the small shawl e, is pink with blue flowers. The fringe in each case matches.

Flowers in the bouquet, f, are yellow and pink.

174

Knekowvak

No. 174 is a blue-eyed, fair-haired gentleman named Knekowvak.   He is
clothed all in white with brown belt and black boots.   The dark coat, *a*, sketched
at right of the doll is plum colored with pink cuffs to match the underlining of
the cape, the tassels and the plain part of the trimming; rickrack braid and buttons, blue; yellow belt to match the design in the corner of the cape.   The crown
of cap is orange; feather and brim, green; buckle, blue.

The remaining coat, *b*, is white with orange cuffs and greenish brown trimmings.   The cap evidently goes with this coat.

No. 175, Hueulskie, wears a white blouse embroidered in plum and green
with a touch of yellow and red at the neck opening; green, red and black striped
sash at waist.   The outer skirt, or apron, is red with plain bands in green and
fancy bands in blue, over a white underskirt.

The contrivance for carrying pails of water, *a*, evidently is meant to wear
over this blouse, for the extra sleeve is of the same pattern and coloring.

The white blouse *b*, sketched underneath this carrying contrivance is trimmed
with sleeve bands in black over an orange background, the main part of the
sleeves embroidered in green and lavender.   The jug has a white background
with designs in green and lavender.   A strand of blue, and one of red beads
decorate the neckline.   Separate shoes are lavender.

The garment at upper right, *c*, consists of a sleeveless jacket of white wool
trimmed with brown and red, and a blouse similar to the one just described, and

175.

Hueulskie

Hueulskie from Poland; water carrier (a); blouse and pitcher (b); sleeveless jacket and blouse (c); purse (d); headgear (e); jacket (f).

a loose red and black cloth girdle. The purse, *d*, meant to be slipped over the head, is rainbow-hued over a background of white.

The headgear, *e*, is medium blue with orange design.

The jacket with sleeves is pale green with black fur edging, and trimming in brown with blue dots.

Huculski, doll No. 176, has brown hair and eyes. He wears a white blouse trimmed with a design in black and purple-red, high-lighted with tiny spots of blue and edged with purple-red banding. He carries a muff with the same coloring as the blouse trimming. Knickers are plain purple-red. Brown moccasins are laced over white socks.

Coat, *a*, and hat, at upper right of the figure match the knickers in coloring. Feather trimming on front of coat is white with blue shading, matching the trimming on the blouse of the doll.

The extra jacket, *b*, is white with black fur around the edges and over the sleeve tops. The rest of the trimming is green, high-lighted with pink; tassels, pink.

Kurpiouskie is the name of the female figure No. 177. Her blouse is white with embroidered trimming to match the pink-figured apron. The skirt is orange, and both apron and skirt are trimmed with black lace-like embroidery.

The costume at the right of the doll, *a*, consists of a white blouse with pink lace trimming, a plum-colored bodice trimmed with green rickrack braid, and a

176.

Huculski

a.

b.

The male doll Huculski has brown hair and eyes. Shown with him are a flaring coat (a); and a jacket from his wardrobe.

white skirt and apron with designs in pink. The apron is trimmed in yellow with black outline, black trimming on skirt; plum-colored boots.

The upper part of a costume with baby, *b*, consists of a white blouse trimmed with pink embroidery to match the flowers in the green shawl in which the baby is wrapped. The infant is fair-haired and wears a red dress with a white ruffle at the neck.

A short jacket, *c*, sketched underneath this shawl-and-baby outfit is of plum color trimmed with tiny flowers in red with green foliage.

The jacket, *d*, at extreme upper right also is plum-colored, with pink lace collar and cuffs and yoke showing at neckline. Jacket trimmings are pink and yellow, with designs just above cuffs and on the pocket in yellow.

The separate skirt and apron, *e*, have the same colors as the complete costume next the doll.

177.

Kurpiouskie

Kurpiouskie and a separate dress with boots (a).

Scarf headdress, *f*, at left of the separate skirt is yellow with red and black trimming, and the headgear, *g*, at right of the skirt is white with red trimming and embroidery. The bouquet is of variegated flowers, red, blue, yellow and lavender.

No. 178, Kasurbskie, has blue eyes and dark hair. Her costume is white with blue, orange, lavender, yellow and pink trimmings. The stars on the sleeve are pink with black dots in center; beads, orange. The wide pleated skirt is trimmed at the bottom with blue and pink rickrack braid. There are pink and blue stars on the bottom of the apron, alternating with designs in blue. Stripes above this design and around the apron are pink. Green sandals are laced over white stockings.

Kurpiouskie's blouse, shawl, baby (b); spencer (c); jacket (d); and matching skirt (e); headgear (f and g).

178

Kasurbskie

Kasurbskie has blue eyes and dark hair, wears green sandals. Separate costume (a); blouse (b); headgear (c).

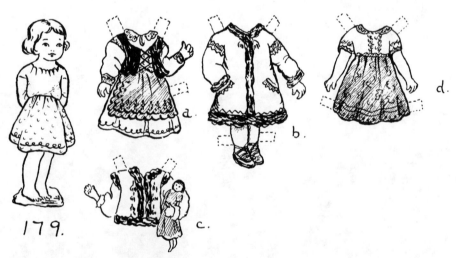

Fair-haired Polish doll, only a little over two inches tall. Dress with apron (a); coat (b); jacket with doll (c); every-day dress (d).

Costume *a* at right of the doll consists of a white blouse with pink and blue trimming; bodice of pink with designs in blue; a pink skirt with blue and orange trimming; and a white apron elaborately trimmed in pink and blue. The white headgear also is trimmed in pink and blue. The separate hat at the left of the outfit just described is white with lavender trimming.

The same coloring as that of the apron is seen in the extra blouse, *b*, except that the bodice is of dark blue, showing a vest of orange and blue stripes. The many strands of beads are in orange, blue, pink, lavender and green.

The hat, *c*, with large bow and streamers is adorned with orange poppies. The bow and streamer at the left are green edged with pink, and the bow and streamer at right are dark red, purple and green. The head scarf is orange with blue dots.

The tiny fair-haired little girl, No. 179, two and one-fourth inches high, looks like a doll. She wears a white blouse and pink skirt edged with black. Costume *a* consists of a white, pink trimmed blouse with plum colored bodice. Pink apron and blue skirt are trimmed with designs in black. The longer coat, *b*, is white trimmed with light brown fur; the sleeveless short jacket, *c*, is pink trimmed with light brown fur, over a white blouse with pink ruffles at the cuff. The doll in the child's arm is dressed in red to match the skirt of the little dress *d* at the extreme right. The waist of the latter is white trimmed with pink, and there are blue dots in the center of the waist trimming.

These Polish dolls are illustrated with the thought that collectors might be encouraged to correspond with friends abroad who may be able to locate other European paper dolls in native costume, thus helping to perpetuate the history of these colorful ensembles which are fast becoming things of the past.

Chapter XV

Paper Dolls in Newspapers and Magazines

FOR the past one hundred years or more newspapers and magazines have published paper dolls. Sometimes the dolls tell a story. As a supplement to a Chicago Sunday paper in 1901, shortly after the Spanish-American war, a series of paper dolls was issued to tell of the people in the Phillippines. There were a Tagalog girl, a Macabebe warrior, a Philippine woman, two Cuban ladies, a cock-fighter, a patriot and the Cuban General Gomez.

Back in in 1911 the Hearst Sunday papers contributed paper dolls that today are collectors items, for they represented noted actresses of the period, among them Geraldine Farrar with costumes for Mme. Butterfly and Marguerite, and Maude Adams with costumes for Chanticleer, Peter Pan, etc.

Among the largest and best of the Sunday supplement series of paper dolls was that presented by *The Sunday Herald* of Boston during the years 1895 and 1896. Mrs. Willie H. Armstrong of Austin, Texas, has a large collection of these dolls' dresses, together with the two figures offered at that time, a blonde and a brunette "lady." Mrs. Armstrong's brunette is illustrated here under the name "Mrs. B. S. Herald," No. 180.

The "Ladies' Yachting Toilette," No. 181, at the right of the doll is Plate No. 11 in the series and was issued June 9, 1895. Shaded parts represent light blue. Trimming is white with a fine yellow edge, and the hat is white with a yellow buckle on blue ribbon trimming.

No. 182, Plate No. 28 in the original series, is described as a "Ladies' Redingote Costume." It is an uncut sheet and shows the dress, hat, rear view of costume "in small" and the information: "A duplicate of the 'Model Figure' will be mailed to subscribers of the Boston *Sunday Herald* upon receipt of four cents (two 2 cent stamps) to cover postage and mailing expenses." Directions for cutting are under the dress, and, in very fine type at lower left of the sheet the notation: "Copyright, 1895, by G. M. Buex & Co., N. Y. Lith." The costume is in two shades of green.

Collectors who have uncut sheets are fortunate, for not only does the hat come with the dress, but the back of the costume is shown "in small," thus enabling would-be costumers to have an accurate all-round picture. The exact date and the plate number also are given.

The striped dress, No. 183, a walking costume, is dated May 19, 1895, Plate No. 8. On this sheet additional information is offered. It is stated that a pattern for the outfit may be obtained, and explains that the waist is called a jacket basque, the skirt an organ pipe. The costume is light gray with a deeper stripe in the material, and dark gray revers. The front of the waist, and the ribbon trimming down the skirt, are foliage green. A white gloved hand carries a black umbrella with rose color just underneath the handle. Rose colored flowers decorate a gray hat. No. 184, at the right of this walking outfit, is a white afternoon gown.

LADIES' YACHTING TOILETTE.

180

181.

Boston Sunday Herald "Model Figure" of 1895; at the right, the "Ladies Yachting Toilette," plate number 11 of the series, issued June 9, 1895.

Ladies' Redingote Costume, The Sunday Herald's weekly Costume
Plate No. 28, October 13, 1895.

At left, a striped dress; right, white afternoon gown.

The costume with square revers, No. 185, called an English jacket suit, is brown with gray flecks in the material. It has a white dickey, blue lapels to match the blue ribbon in the brown hat, and the gloves are pale yellow.

The lounging dress, No. 186, is pink trimmed with white lace, and the baby in arms, a little blonde, wears the traditional white. This outfit was contributed by Mrs. Lake.

The "Ladies' Street Toilette with Marie Antoinette Fur Set," No. 187, in place on a doll, is gray with white ermine fur, and a deeper shade of gray feathers on a light gray hat. This was the issue of October 20th, 1895, original plate No. 29.

No. 188 is a "Ladies Demi-evening Toilette." It consists of a revered basque made with a pink rose and green leaves print, and a shirred white blousette shows at the opening in the front. The skirt is plain green. The original plate is not numbered, but the date is February 23, 1896.

Sometimes the year is not printed on the plate. Such is the case with No. 189. Since the original plate number is low—No. 30—it probably is 1895. The date of the month is October 27th, and is labelled "Ladies' Opera Cloak." It is a pale brocaded green lined with pale pink and decorated with white boa feathers. Dress and fan are white.

185

186

To the left, English Jacket Suit of brown with gray flecks in the material. It has white dickey, blue lapels to match the blue ribbon in the brown hat. At right, lounging dress of pink, trimmed with white lace. The baby is blond-haired, and is dressed in the traditional white of that day.

At the left, "Ladies' Street Toilette with Marie Antoinette Fur Set," in The Sunday Herald (Boston) of October 20, 1895. At right, "Ladies' Demi-evening Toilette," with revered basque made with a pink rose and green leaves print, and a shirred white blousette with opening at the front. The skirt is plain green. Date is February 23, 1896.

At left, "Ladies' Opera Coat," probably 1895; at right, red dress with light brown fur muff and trimming. Both from The Sunday Herald series.

No. 190 is a red dress with light brown fur muff and trimming. This was a cutout, therefore unlabelled, as are the rest of the ''lady'' costumes described.

The two afternoon or evening dresses, Nos. 191 and 192, are in the following colors: left, a pink blouse with dark gray skirt and ribbon sash and white gloves; right, pink with white lace trimmings; white bodice and gloves. The lace yoke is edged with a narrow strip of gray fur.

Sports costumes are as follows: bicycle outfit, No. 193, light tan with white blouse and belt, black shoes, dark gray spats and light gray gloves; bathing costume, No. 194, electric blue trimmed with white braid, white collar and cuffs, a red sash, and black shoes and stockings; tennis outfit, No. 195, white with blue stripes, white collar, tie, belt and gloves; and the riding costume, No. 196, is dark gray with a white shirtwaist, black necktie and yellow gloves.

It is but natural that other newspapers, not to be outdone by their competitors, should also present Sunday supplement paper dolls at about the same time. In 1895 *The Boston Globe* brought out what they called an Art Supplement. One series, dated June 2, 1895, was called the bridal party, although the dolls depicted were children. These came in two sheets, approximately seven and a half inches by eleven and one-fourth inches, each sheet folded in the

191   192.

Two afternoon or evening dresses from The Sunday Herald series. The left one in the
illustration has a pink blouse with dark gray skirt and ribbon sash and white gloves.
The one at the right is pink with white lace trimmings, white bodice, and gloves. The
lace yoke is edged with a narrow strip of gray fur.

193 194

Sports costume in The Sunday Herald series, showing bicycle outfit and bathing suit.

The Sunday Herald sports costumes included the tennis
outfit at the left and the riding costume at the right.

middle. (See sketches.) No. 197 shows the bride, her wedding and traveling dresses on one side of the fold, and the best man, a bathing suit and a Fauntleroy jacket on the other side. The extremely youthful bride has brown eyes and hair, a white petticoat and corset cover trimmed at the neckline with blue, red stockings and brown boots. Her wedding gown is pale yellow, the veil white; gloves and flowers match the veil. The traveling dress has a yellow skirt with pink ribbon trimmings, and the blouse matches the ribbons on the skirt. Collar and ribbons over shoulders are yellow, and the yoke is white with pink dots.

The equally youthful best man also has brown eyes and hair. His blouse is white with a pink ribbon tie at the neck, pink sash, green trousers, black stockings and brown shoes. His Fauntleroy jacket is medium blue with white collar, the latter trimmed with lighter blue, and white ruffles trim his cuffs. The bathing suit is gay with pink and white stripes, white collar and cuffs edged with pink and a pink tassel at the neck. Slippers are brown. Evidently he felt the need of a swim after the ceremony.

The second sheet (No. 198) illustrating the groom and bridesmaid also suggests a trip to the water. The yachting suit belonging to the groom consists of a white middy with blue collar and cuffs, blue sailor pants and red and white striped trousers. The doll itself wears a little-boy white blouse with blue trimmings and tie, short yellow pants, red belt, black stockings and brown shoes. His evening dress is typical except for the short trousers befitting his tender years.

The bridesmaid is a brunette, a buxom corseted figure, although evidently not more than ten years of age. The corset is a startling electric blue, the petticoat yellow trimmed with red, and a white chemise with red trimming peeps out from above the corset. Her tea gown is green over a white slip, yoke and ribbon sash are pink, and the sleeves and waist trimmed with white lace. The bathing suit is deep pink with white trimmings. Stockings match, and the slippers are brown. It is presumed the young couple invited their best man and bridesmaid to join their honeymoon party at the shore.

The set is reproduced here through the courtesy of Mrs. Lake.

One of the earliest magazines to print paper dolls was *Godey's Lady's Book*, edited by Sarah Jane Hale, published in Philadelphia. On page 9 of the November, 1859, issue we have "Diagrams for dressing Children—for little girls who read Godey." (See illustration No. 199). The "diagrams" or paper dolls are given in black and white. The identical costumes, but in color, appear on page 6. Colors are as follows: *a.* yellow skirt with red rose design to match flowers in yellow bonnet; yellow ruffle around front and bottom of basque, the latter lace-trimmed at sleeves and lower edge; green trimming and ribbons on crown of bonnet, and green bow on basque at neck line; white, lace-edged pantalettes: *b*, green dress, orange basque, both trimmed with yellow material on which has been sewn a row of orange buttons; white ruffles at neck and sleeves: *c*, yellow lace-ruffled dress with orange bows: *d*, yellow, orange and blue plaid is painted in, for there is no indication of plaid in uncolored sketch; lace trimmings and lace-trimmed pantalettes; orange colored cap: *e* consists of a green basque with fichu and panniers of the same plaid as shown in d. The skirt is orange with a black band around the lower part. Apron (caught up in hand) and ruffle around sleeve are white, the latter trimmed with an orange

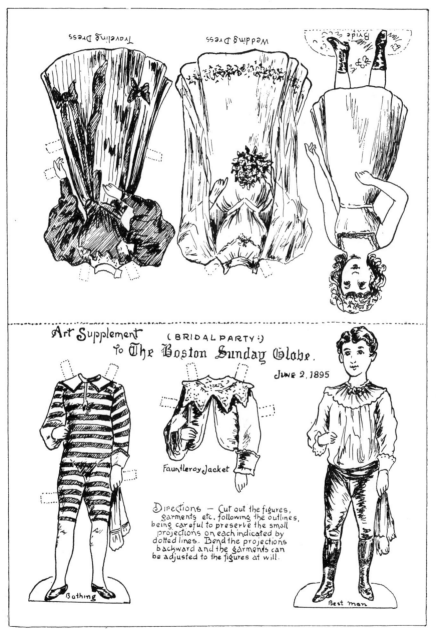

Traveling Dress

Wedding Dress

Bride etc.

Art Supplement (BRIDAL PARTY:)
to The Boston Sunday Globe.

June 2, 1895

Fauntleroy Jacket

Directions — Cut out the figures,
garments etc. following the outlines,
being careful to preserve the small
projections on each indicated by
dotted lines. Bend the projections
backward and the garments can
be adjusted to the figures at will.

Bathing

Best man

197

The Boston Globe in 1895 brought out a series called an "Art Supplement." The above shows part of a "Bridal Party," though all the dolls shown are obviously children.

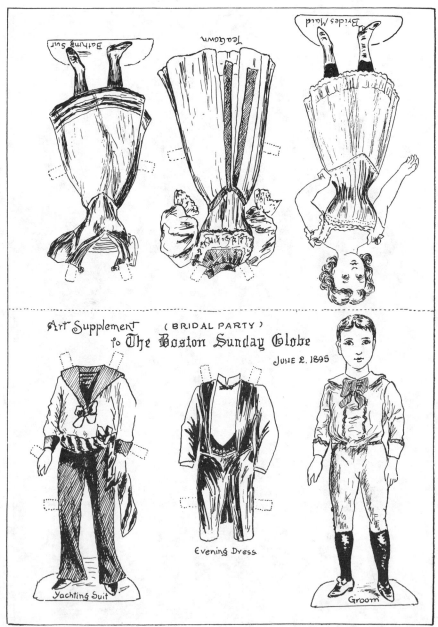

198.

The groom and the bridesmaid in the Bridal Party shown on the preceding
page, where the bride and the best man are seen.

Diagram for dressing children, published by Godey's Lady's Book, one of the first magazines to print paper dolls. The above were published in the November 1859 issue, and the dolls were in black and white. The identical costumes, however appeared on another page of the same issue in color. A description of the colored costumes appears on page 200.

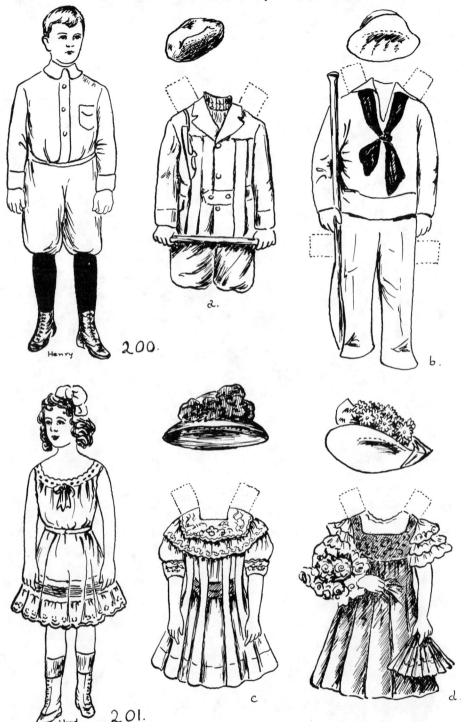

Henry and Lloyd Lane, Reprinted by special permission from the Ladies Home Journal, Copyright 1908. The Curtis Publishing Company.

colored ribbon bow: *f*, blue coat and cap, the latter trimmed with a white feather, below which is an orange rosette to match orange bands on a yellow skirt; white sleeves, collar and pantalettes.

Old copies of *Godey's Lady's Book,* including the issue containing the paper dolls just described, may be seen in the Rare Books Division of the Library of Congress, Washington, D. C. The sketches in this book were taken from the magazine in the possession of Miss Howard.

Starting in the late nineteenth century, women's periodicals such as the *Delineator* published paper dolls and thereafter continued to issue them from time to time. And paper dolls were advertised in magazines as far back as 1858. Mrs. Lillian S. Smith, who recently purchased the well-known Humpty Dumpty Doll Hospital of Redondo Beach, California, writes of an advertisement of this kind which appeared in *Peterson's Magazine* for the year 1858. It reads:

"Children's Holiday Sport—Cinderella and the little glass slipper, with magic changes. Price 15 cents—prettier than all the paper dolls. Changes, Cinderella, The Prince, The Fairy God-Mother, and different costumes to each, with the beautiful carriage she went to the ball in, beautifully colored, all for 15 cents. Just published by J. E. Tilton, Salem, Mass."

A prolific period for magazine paper dolls was between the years 1909 and 1924. The *Delineator* offered some well-designed "Round-Base Paper Dolls" by Carolyn Chester. These included historic costumes for a wedding of 1863. The same magazine also published dolls and clothes printed both back and front. Grace Drayton illustrated, in paper doll form, the old fairy tales for the *Pictorial Review.* The Hader Sisters made some novel dancing paper dolls for *Good Housekeeping.* The *Womans Home Companion, John Martin's Book* and many children's magazines also carried paper dolls. The *Ladies' Home Journal* was particularly prolific in bringing out paper dolls. Frances Hunter designed twin baby dolls for one issue and in another showed them grown older. In 1923 Gertrude Kay illustrated stories by Sarah Addington in a series of cut-outs. Sheila Young made two long series of paper dolls for the *Ladies' Home Journal* —the Lettie Lane series, which started in the October, 1908, issue and ran through July, 1915, and the Betty Bonnet series, which appeared from September, 1915, to September, 1918. The series is so interesting that many persons, not necessarily collectors, have saved the dolls. Those illustrated are the property of Mrs. Arthur R. Leiby of Lexington, Massachusetts. They are reprinted by special permission from the *Ladies' Home Journal.* Copyright 1908, the Curtis Publishing Company.

"Henry" wears a white suit, black shoes, tie and stockings. His skating costume, including cap, is light gray, and his boating outfit, white.

"Lloyd Lane" is dressed in white underwear, shoes, socks and hair ribbon, Pink ribbon runs through the beading of the underwear at the neckline. Costume *c* is white with a blue ribbon sash and blue trimmings on a white hat. The garden costume, *d*, is light green over a white blouse. In one hand is held a gray fan, in the other, yellow roses. The hat is yellow, trimmed with white daisies.

Through the kindness of the *Ladies' Home Journal* we are able to give a complete and impressive list of the two last named very interesting series.

Chapter XVI

Portrait Paper Dolls—

Six Famous Queens and Martha Washington

A LMOST anyone will agree that portrait paper dolls are the most interesting of all the great family of paper dolls. Individual examples have been given in other chapters, but as a set of portrait dolls, E. S. Tucker's "Six Famous Queens and Martha Washington" are worthy a place of their own. Each queen and Martha Washington were accompanied by three costumes ready cut with tabs to keep them in place on the doll. They seem to have been on the market for many years. The earliest set in the writer's knowledge was formerly owned by a woman between eighty and ninety years of age who says she played with them as a youngster. The only name which appears on the box containing the set is that of E. S. Tucker. Collectors who have only one or two of the set will be glad to see the illustrations in this chapter to discover what the remaining dolls look like.

First we have the tragic queen of France, Marie Antoinette, who lived from 1755 to 1793. Little did she realize the truth of the saying "Uneasy lies the head that wears a crown" when at the tender age of fifteen she became the bride of Louis XVI in the year 1770. All the civilized world knows how twenty-three years later, she was sacrificed to the passion of an angry mob, behaving with brave dignity befitting a queen even to the last moment before her execution. When asked at that time if she had anything to say she replied: "I was your queen, you have taken away my crown, a wife, and you killed my husband, a mother and you deprived me of my children. My blood alone remains; take it, but do not let me suffer long." The spectators at the execution were awed by the expression of her face at the moment of death; it was as though she beheld some wonderful vision.

Paper dolls may seem trivial to many persons, but when they help keep alive the memory of brave men and women and personalize the lives of those who have made and are making history quite aside from their costume value, they serve a worthwhile purpose.

The doll in question, Marie Antoinette, shows a white boudoir costume, white slippers, pearl necklace and white powdered wig, and she stands on a carpet or tile of the same color.

The Court Robe, which is blue with a design in gold color, is lavishly lined with ermine. Under the robe is a white gown with yellow yoke decorated with jewelry emphasizing pearls.

Marie's walking gown is white with greenish blue ribbon bow and streamers at the point of the bodice. Roses in a green basket are held in one hand, a bouquet in the other.

Underdress of the reception gown is white with green trimming, the redin-

E. S. Tucker's "Marie Antoinette" in his set of "Six Famous Queens and Martha Washington." Court robe (a); walking gown (b); reception gown (c).

Reception Robe   a.

Court Robe   b.

c.
Walking Gown

Isabella of Spain 1492   203

"Isabella of Spain" in the E. S. Tucker set, and her gowns.

gote, red-brown. Flowers embroidered on the white ruffle on collar and cuffs and painted on the fan match the redingote. The scarf is white.

The date printed on the doll is 1789, at which time Marie was thirty-two. She had at that time but four years to live.

The paper doll Isabella of Spain is dated 1492, which would make her forty-one years of age when she helped to finance Columbus on his mighty voyage of discovery. She was the daughter of John II of Castile by a second wife, Isabella of Portugal, who later became Queen of Castile, so that when daughter Isabella married Ferdinand V, King of Aragon, the two kingdoms were united under the Royal title of Spain. The couple had five children who helped populate the royal families of Europe. Isabella took an active part in state affairs. A religious fanatic, her administration of justice was not always tempered with mercy, but she did her best to promote the welfare of her country to the time of her death in 1504, at the age of fifty-three.

The paper doll, Isabella, has blue eyes and black hair and a boudoir costume of white. She stands on pale yellow squares outlined in light brown.

The reception robe at upper right of doll is pale yellow, shaded in deeper yellow, with blue-green designs. Jewels which form the trimming are red, and

Reception
Robe

Court
Robe

Louise of Prussia   1797

204

Walking Gown

The "Six Famous Queens" of E. S. Tucker included "Louise of Prussia," shown above. Reception robe (a); court robe (b); walking gown (c).

on the end of the scarf and around the neckline of the basque the jewels are placed on a green background.

Isabella's court robe (upper right) is royal red, lined with ermine, and finished with an ermine cape, while the gown showing beneath is white, trimmed at the neckline and center of the bodice with yellow and red gems. A casket held in the hands we suppose contains the jewels intended to help Columbus.

The elegant walking costume at the lower right of the doll is in black, yellow and white, the redingote in black with sleeve linings and trimming in yellow, a yellow girdle and white dress, pearl trimmings on bodice and on brown arm bands and cuff of sleeve.

Louise of Prussia (1716-1810) was made queen in 1797, when she and her husband, Wilhelm III, were crowned. She bore ten children in her happily married life, and was her husbands constant advisor, especially during the difficult time preceding Napoleons capture of Prussia. Louise had been very sad for some time over conditions in France, and wept bitterly over the death of Marie Antoinette. When she died there was great mourning, for she had been very much beloved by her people.

The period of the French Revolution was reflected in the clothes worn at that time. They were simple in material and cut, gowns short-waisted and footwear without heels. Hair-do was not elaborate and short hair fashionable except for court attire

The paper doll of Queen Louise of Prussia shows blue eyes and light brown hair, a dainty white boudoir costume with a bow and blue ribbon streamers down the front; yellow slippers, and a yellow band with a star in the middle of her simply curled hair. The scarf about her chin is white, although the real doll supposed to represent Louise has a blue scarf, and is often called "the blue scarf doll."

The walking gown is pale gray with a narrow white scarf tied at the neck and hanging down the front of the costume almost to the narrow ruffle around the border of the skirt. A yellow shawl and belt is set off by dark gray fingerless gloves, and slippers to match the gloves.

The reception robe is a simple white dress with pearls at neck, sleeve and hem-line, and a long blue ribbon sash. A touch of yellow at neck, sleeves and hem of skirt, and red roses held in the hand, add just the right finish to this lovely simple gown.

The court robe is, of course, less plain. A golden crown matches the yellow design in the bottom of the white dress and the sides of the royal purple overdress. A purple mantle held over the arm is lined with ermine. Jewels in crown match mantle and overdress, the latter completed with a yellow girdle. The center design of the necklace is a ruby surrounded by pearls. The rest of the necklace is alternate red and white jewels. A white lace veil flutters from the crown. At the waist is a purple jewel with yellow pendants attached.

The paper doll is dated 1797, the year in which Louise was made Queen.

Queen Elizabeth of England was the last of the Tudor dynasty. Of her seventy years of life (1533-1603) she reigned as Queen forty-five years, prosperous years for England, despite wars and threats of wars. She was responsible for the reestablishment and maintenance of the Protestant faith in her country,

Elizabeth of England   1538   205   a   Walking Gown

Reception Robe   b. Court Robe   c

"Elizabeth of England," in the E. S. Tucker series.
Walking gown (a); reception robe (b); court robe (c).

for expansion on sea and land, and great cultural growth. This was the age of Shakespeare and Bacon and Spenser; the age of discovery; the time when Sir Walter Raleigh founded the first British settlement in North America; when Drake and Hawkins made their discoveries, and The East India Company, which later founded a new empire for England, was granted its first charter from Elizabeth. History has established her as a great queen.

The paper doll representative of Queen Elizabeth is dressed in a white boudoir costume, the outer garment caught up at the sleeves and chest with yellow bows which match the mirror in hand. There are pearls in the hair and about her neck. The pendant in the upper necklace is red with a touch of light blue. Although the queen was reputed to have red hair, the paper doll shows reddish brown.

The walking costume at right of Elizabeth is royal purple caught up with a yellow and orange girdle. Narrow bands of yellow, center-striped with orange, divide the sleeve into five puffs and the same trimming is on the bodice and the hemline of the skirt. Jewels on the bodice are yellow and purple with a touch of orange. The white under-skirt is bordered by a design in yellow, and the gloves are of the same color. A stiff, starched white ruff accompanies all three of the separate costumes.

The overdress of the court robe is royal red trimmed and lined with ermine, and caught about the waist with a yellow girdle which matches the design bordering the white underdress. Pearls and rubies bedeck the crown and hair. There are pearls about the bodice and wrist.

Elizabeth's reception robe is yellow lined with white and caught up at the oversleeves with white ribbons to match the underdress. The latter is trimmed with yellow banding centered with a row of pearls and the bodice is elaborately trimmed with varicolored gems. The center of a white fan is also bejeweled.

The doll is dated at the time of her ascension to the throne, 1558.

Victoria was one of the greatest of England's queens. Succeeding to the throne in 1837, at the age of eighteen, she reigned for sixty-four years, and during that time England grew and prospered. Walter Besant, in his book "Fifty Years Ago," published in 1888, gives a good picture of England at the time of Victoria's coronation. He says:

"In the year 1837—I shall repeat this remark several times, because I wish to impress the fact upon everybody—we were still, to all intents and purposes, in the eighteenth century. As yet the country was untouched by that American influence which is now filling all peoples with new ideas. Rank was still held in the ancient reverence; religion was still that of the eighteenth-century Church; the rights of labour were not yet recognized; there were no railways to speak of; nobody travelled except the rich; their own country was unknown to the people; the majority of country people could not read or write; the good old discipline of Father Stick and his children, Cat-o'-Nine-Tails, Rope's-end, Strap, Birch, Ferule, and Cane, was wholesomely maintained; landlords, manufacturers, and employers of all kinds did what they pleased with their own; and the Blue Ribbon was unheard of."

In the short space of fifty years after the reign of Victoria began amazing changes had taken place. For a hundred and fifty years there had been no loyalty, no love by the oppressed people for their sovereign. How could there be? They were abject slaves. Now they were beginning to stand upright; they had a voice in the government, England had expanded beyond her wildest dreams. The Queen was fulfilling with all her heart and soul the promise she made as a

Victoria of England 1837

Reception Robe

Walking Gown b.

Court Robe c

Tucker's "Victoria of England." Reception robe (a); walking gown (b); court robe (c).

young girl and word came to her that she was to be a ruler of a great people—"I will be good." Victoria was fortunate in that she was surrounded by the ablest advisors of her day, and, in ascending the throne at so early an age, the people were drawn to her and grew to love her more and more as the years ripened the girl into maturity. Except for the Crimean War and the Indian Mutiny, her reign was peaceful. She was born in 1819 and died in 1901, four years after London gaily celebrated her Diamond Jubilee.

There probably were many paper dolls made to represent so famous a person as Victoria, but the only one to come to the attention of the writer is the one in the set under discussion. The doll shows a youthful Victoria with blue eyes and light hair, attired in white for the boudoir except for a strip of pale yellow over the criss-cross design in the petticoat and blue ribbon shirred into eyelets at the neckline and hanging in long streamers down the front. Earrings are blue with a touch of red at the lobe of the ear, and the necklace is in yellow, red and blue. The date on the back of the doll is Victorias coronation year, 1837.

The reception robe at the right of the doll is white brocade with a touch of red and yellow in the otherwise white corsage; pearl jewelry; white glove and fan and trimming around a yellow brocade cape.

The walking gown is light blue with matching sunshade, and light blue lace trims a black shawl.

Victoria's court robe is royal red over a white brocade skirt trimmed with yellow and orange at the bottom, and a yellow waist matches yellow bands on the robe. The latter is edged with ermine. Sleeves, glove and handkerchief are white, matching the lining of the robe. Jewels are red and yellow, and the girdle is yellow.

Margherita of Italy is a little nearer our own time. She was born in 1851 and died in 1926. Her father was Prince Ferdinand of Savoy, Duke of Genoa, and her mother, Princess Elizabeth, daughter of the King of Saxony, the latter an accomplished scholar.

The date printed on the paper doll of Margherita is 1868, the year she was married to her cousin Humbert of Savoy, Prince of Piedmont. Ten years later Margherita was made queen through the ascension to the throne of her husband, who succeeded Victor Emanuel II. The queen endeared herself in the hearts of her people not only by her charming personality and sweet disposition, but also by her charitable works. On one occasion she saved the life of her husband who was about to be attacked by an assassin by throwing a bouquet of flowers in the face of the latter. An anarchist finally murdered Humbert in 1900.

Margherita's negligee is pale blue lined with pink to match the collar. It is tied in front with long blue ribbons. The petticoat with its embroidered double flounce is white with blue ribbon beading. The queen has blue eyes and yellow hair, and the pearl necklace matches the star in headband.

Margherita's walking gown is white with blue ribbon and pearls for trimming, and a blue sunshade is carried in a white gloved hand.

The court robe is pale green over a white dress embroidered at the bottom. Bodice and sleeves are decorated with pearls. White gloves and a white ostrich feather fan complete the outfit.

A royal red cape lined with white fur to match the white dress forms the reception robe. Ropes of pearls at the neck add a touch of elegance.

a.
Court Costume

b.
Walking Gown

207

1868

Margherita of Italy

Reception Robe

Tucker's "Margherita of Italy." Court costume (a); walking gown (b); reception robe (c).

Martha Washington, wife of America's first president, was born Martha Dandridge in the year 1732. Colonel Daniel Parke Custis won her hand when she was but seventeen years of age, and by him she had four children, two of whom died in childhood. Two children, Martha and John, survived their father's early death and were taken to Mt. Vernon shortly after their mother's marriage to Colonel George Washington in 1759.

When Washington was elected commander-in-chief of the armies of his country, Lady Washington, as she was called, accompanied him on his missions whenever possible, and after his election to the presidency in 1787, she continued to help in every way possible, entertaining with gracious ease.

Martha's state robe is white with ribbons and mitts. A pink underskirt makes a pretty contrast.

Mrs. Sarah Jane Hale in her book *Distinguished Women* has this to say of Martha Washington:

> "In person Mrs. Washington was well formed, though somewhat below the middle size. A portrait, taken previous to her marriage, shows that she must have been very handsome in her youth; and she retained a comeliness of countenance, as well as a dignified grace of manner, during life. In her home she was the presiding genius that kept action and order in perfect harmony; a wife in whom the heart of her husband could safely trust."

A few years ago an interesting illustrated booklet was written by Aline Bernstein and published by Howell, Soskin, Inc. containing two paper dolls of Martha Washington with eight separate costumes in color. It tells briefly of the life and times of America's first leading lady, and illustrates utensils, furniture, etc. used at Mount Vernon. Booklets like this, instructive as well as entertaining, should be in the hands of every school child.

They were a devoted couple, and it was a great blow to Martha when her husband passed on. She was sitting at his bedside at the time—December 14, 1799—trying to resign herself to the inevitable, and when it happened, she said simply " 'Tis well; all is over now; I shall soon follow him; I have no more trials to pass through." Martha had already lost a son, John, aged twenty-seven, in the service of his country, and her namesake, Martha, had died in 1770. Three years after her husband's death she joined him in the Great Beyond together with others of that distinguished company whose memory always will remain green in the hearts of a grateful people.

Most of us have a mental picture of Martha Washington as an old lady, for the greater number of portraits and statuettes were made in her mature years, but in the Tucker set of paper dolls she is shown as a slim young woman. Her eyes are dark, her wig powdered, and she wears a white boudoir cap. Her sack is pink with a design in a darker shade. It is tied at the front and sleeves with matching ribbons, and has a white collar edged with a narrow pink ruffle, the sleeve finished with white lace or embroidery. Her petticoat is white. The doll is dated 1775.

Martha's walking dress is largely in green and white, the overdress green with a white fichu under the green cape or collar of her bodice. The skirt is white with a design in pink, green, and a touch of yellow. Accessories are a green bag and mitts, the former with pink lining and embroidery.

a. Walking Dress

b. State Robe

Reception Gown c.

Martha Washington 1775

208.

"Martha Washington" in the E. S. Tucker set. Walking dress (a); state robe (b); reception gown (c).

Paper Doll Series by Sheila Young

Issued by the Ladies' Home Journal

October, 1908 to September, 1918

Paper Doll Series by Sheila Young in Ladies Home Journal

(Continued from preceding page)

Index

A CATALOG OF SELECTED
DOVER BOOKS
IN ALL FIELDS OF INTEREST

A CATALOG OF SELECTED DOVER BOOKS IN ALL FIELDS OF INTEREST

DRAWINGS OF REMBRANDT, edited by Seymour Slive. Updated Lippmann, Hofstede de Groot edition, with definitive scholarly apparatus. All portraits, biblical sketches, landscapes, nudes. Oriental figures, classical studies, together with selection of work by followers. 550 illustrations. Total of 630pp. 9⅛ × 12¼.
21485-0, 21486-9 Pa., Two-vol. set $25.00

GHOST AND HORROR STORIES OF AMBROSE BIERCE, Ambrose Bierce. 24 tales vividly imagined, strangely prophetic, and decades ahead of their time in technical skill: "The Damned Thing," "An Inhabitant of Carcosa," "The Eyes of the Panther," "Moxon's Master," and 20 more. 199pp. 5⅜ × 8½. 20767-6 Pa. $3.95

ETHICAL WRITINGS OF MAIMONIDES, Maimonides. Most significant ethical works of great medieval sage, newly translated for utmost precision, readability. Laws Concerning Character Traits, Eight Chapters, more. 192pp. 5⅜ × 8½.
24522-5 Pa. $4.50

THE EXPLORATION OF THE COLORADO RIVER AND ITS CANYONS, J. W. Powell. Full text of Powell's 1,000-mile expedition down the fabled Colorado in 1869. Superb account of terrain, geology, vegetation, Indians, famine, mutiny, treacherous rapids, mighty canyons, during exploration of last unknown part of continental U.S. 400pp. 5⅜ × 8½. 20094-9 Pa. $6.95

HISTORY OF PHILOSOPHY, Julián Marías. Clearest one-volume history on the market. Every major philosopher and dozens of others, to Existentialism and later. 505pp. 5⅜ × 8½. 21739-6 Pa. $8.50

ALL ABOUT LIGHTNING, Martin A. Uman. Highly readable non-technical survey of nature and causes of lightning, thunderstorms, ball lightning, St. Elmo's Fire, much more. Illustrated. 192pp. 5⅜ × 8½. 25237-X Pa. $5.95

SAILING ALONE AROUND THE WORLD, Captain Joshua Slocum. First man to sail around the world, alone, in small boat. One of great feats of seamanship told in delightful manner. 67 illustrations. 294pp. 5⅜ × 8½. 20326-3 Pa. $4.95

LETTERS AND NOTES ON THE MANNERS, CUSTOMS AND CONDITIONS OF THE NORTH AMERICAN INDIANS, George Catlin. Classic account of life among Plains Indians: ceremonies, hunt, warfare, etc. 312 plates. 572pp. of text. 6⅛ × 9¼. 22118-0, 22119-9 Pa. Two-vol. set $15.90

ALASKA: The Harriman Expedition, 1899, John Burroughs, John Muir, et al. Informative, engrossing accounts of two-month, 9,000-mile expedition. Native peoples, wildlife, forests, geography, salmon industry, glaciers, more. Profusely illustrated. 240 black-and-white line drawings. 124 black-and-white photographs. 3 maps. Index. 576pp. 5⅜ × 8½. 25109-8 Pa. $11.95

THE BOOK OF BEASTS: Being a Translation from a Latin Bestiary of the Twelfth Century, T. H. White. Wonderful catalog real and fanciful beasts: manticore, griffin, phoenix, amphivius, jaculus, many more. White's witty erudite commentary on scientific, historical aspects. Fascinating glimpse of medieval mind. Illustrated. 296pp. 5⅜ × 8¼. (Available in U.S. only) 24609-4 Pa. $5.95

FRANK LLOYD WRIGHT: ARCHITECTURE AND NATURE With 160 Illustrations, Donald Hoffmann. Profusely illustrated study of influence of nature—especially prairie—on Wright's designs for Fallingwater, Robie House, Guggenheim Museum, other masterpieces. 96pp. 9¼ × 10¾. 25098-9 Pa. $7.95

FRANK LLOYD WRIGHT'S FALLINGWATER, Donald Hoffmann. Wright's famous waterfall house: planning and construction of organic idea. History of site, owners, Wright's personal involvement. Photographs of various stages of building. Preface by Edgar Kaufmann, Jr. 100 illustrations. 112pp. 9¼ × 10.
23671-4 Pa. $7.95

YEARS WITH FRANK LLOYD WRIGHT: Apprentice to Genius, Edgar Tafel. Insightful memoir by a former apprentice presents a revealing portrait of Wright the man, the inspired teacher, the greatest American architect. 372 black-and-white illustrations. Preface. Index. vi + 228pp. 8¼ × 11. 24801-1 Pa. $9.95

THE STORY OF KING ARTHUR AND HIS KNIGHTS, Howard Pyle. Enchanting version of King Arthur fable has delighted generations with imaginative narratives of exciting adventures and unforgettable illustrations by the author. 41 illustrations. xviii + 313pp. 6⅛ × 9¼. 21445-1 Pa. $5.95

THE GODS OF THE EGYPTIANS, E. A. Wallis Budge. Thorough coverage of numerous gods of ancient Egypt by foremost Egyptologist. Information on evolution of cults, rites and gods; the cult of Osiris; the Book of the Dead and its rites; the sacred animals and birds; Heaven and Hell; and more. 956pp. 6⅛ × 9¼.
22055-9, 22056-7 Pa., Two-vol. set $21.90

A THEOLOGICO-POLITICAL TREATISE, Benedict Spinoza. Also contains unfinished *Political Treatise*. Great classic on religious liberty, theory of government on common consent. R. Elwes translation. Total of 421pp. 5⅜ × 8½.
20249-6 Pa. $6.95

INCIDENTS OF TRAVEL IN CENTRAL AMERICA, CHIAPAS, AND YUCATAN, John L. Stephens. Almost single-handed discovery of Maya culture; exploration of ruined cities, monuments, temples; customs of Indians. 115 drawings. 892pp. 5⅜ × 8½. 22404-X, 22405-8 Pa., Two-vol. set $15.90

LOS CAPRICHOS, Francisco Goya. 80 plates of wild, grotesque monsters and caricatures. Prado manuscript included. 183pp. 6⅜ × 9⅜. 22384-1 Pa. $4.95

AUTOBIOGRAPHY: The Story of My Experiments with Truth, Mohandas K. Gandhi. Not hagiography, but Gandhi in his own words. Boyhood, legal studies, purification, the growth of the Satyagraha (nonviolent protest) movement. Critical, inspiring work of the man who freed India. 480pp. 5⅜ × 8½. (Available in U.S. only)
24593-4 Pa. $6.95

ILLUSTRATED DICTIONARY OF HISTORIC ARCHITECTURE, edited by Cyril M. Harris. Extraordinary compendium of clear, concise definitions for over 5,000 important architectural terms complemented by over 2,000 line drawings. Covers full spectrum of architecture from ancient ruins to 20th-century Modernism. Preface. 592pp. 7½ × 9⅝. 24444-X Pa. $14.95

THE NIGHT BEFORE CHRISTMAS, Clement Moore. Full text, and woodcuts from original 1848 book. Also critical, historical material. 19 illustrations. 40pp. 4⅝ × 6. 22797-9 Pa. $2.50

THE LESSON OF JAPANESE ARCHITECTURE: 165 Photographs, Jiro Harada. Memorable gallery of 165 photographs taken in the 1930's of exquisite Japanese homes of the well-to-do and historic buildings. 13 line diagrams. 192pp. 8⅜ × 11¼. 24778-3 Pa. $8.95

THE AUTOBIOGRAPHY OF CHARLES DARWIN AND SELECTED LETTERS, edited by Francis Darwin. The fascinating life of eccentric genius composed of an intimate memoir by Darwin (intended for his children); commentary by his son, Francis; hundreds of fragments from notebooks, journals, papers; and letters to and from Lyell, Hooker, Huxley, Wallace and Henslow. xi + 365pp. 5⅜ × 8. 20479-0 Pa. $5.95

WONDERS OF THE SKY: Observing Rainbows, Comets, Eclipses, the Stars and Other Phenomena, Fred Schaaf. Charming, easy-to-read poetic guide to all manner of celestial events visible to the naked eye. Mock suns, glories, Belt of Venus, more. Illustrated. 299pp. 5¼ × 8¼. 24402-4 Pa. $7.95

BURNHAM'S CELESTIAL HANDBOOK, Robert Burnham, Jr. Thorough guide to the stars beyond our solar system. Exhaustive treatment. Alphabetical by constellation: Andromeda to Cetus in Vol. 1; Chamaeleon to Orion in Vol. 2; and Pavo to Vulpecula in Vol. 3. Hundreds of illustrations. Index in Vol. 3. 2,000pp. 6⅛ × 9¼. 23567-X, 23568-8, 23673-0 Pa., Three-vol. set $37.85

STAR NAMES: Their Lore and Meaning, Richard Hinckley Allen. Fascinating history of names various cultures have given to constellations and literary and folkloristic uses that have been made of stars. Indexes to subjects. Arabic and Greek names. Biblical references. Bibliography. 563pp. 5⅜ × 8½. 21079-0 Pa. $7.95

THIRTY YEARS THAT SHOOK PHYSICS: The Story of Quantum Theory, George Gamow. Lucid, accessible introduction to influential theory of energy and matter. Careful explanations of Dirac's anti-particles, Bohr's model of the atom, much more. 12 plates. Numerous drawings. 240pp. 5⅜ × 8½. 24895-X Pa. $4.95

CHINESE DOMESTIC FURNITURE IN PHOTOGRAPHS AND MEASURED DRAWINGS, Gustav Ecke. A rare volume, now affordably priced for antique collectors, furniture buffs and art historians. Detailed review of styles ranging from early Shang to late Ming. Unabridged republication. 161 black-and-white drawings, photos. Total of 224pp. 8⅜ × 11¼. (Available in U.S. only) 25171-3 Pa. $12.95

VINCENT VAN GOGH: A Biography, Julius Meier-Graefe. Dynamic, penetrating study of artist's life, relationship with brother, Theo, painting techniques, travels, more. Readable, engrossing. 160pp. 5⅜ × 8½. (Available in U.S. only) 25253-1 Pa. $3.95

CATALOG OF DOVER BOOKS

HOW TO WRITE, Gertrude Stein. Gertrude Stein claimed anyone could understand her unconventional writing—here are clues to help. Fascinating improvisations, language experiments, explanations illuminate Stein's craft and the art of writing. Total of 414pp. 4⅝ × 6⅝. 23144-5 Pa. $5.95

ADVENTURES AT SEA IN THE GREAT AGE OF SAIL: Five Firsthand Narratives, edited by Elliot Snow. Rare true accounts of exploration, whaling, shipwreck, fierce natives, trade, shipboard life, more. 33 illustrations. Introduction. 353pp. 5⅜ × 8½. 25177-2 Pa. $7.95

THE HERBAL OR GENERAL HISTORY OF PLANTS, John Gerard. Classic descriptions of about 2,850 plants—with over 2,700 illustrations—includes Latin and English names, physical descriptions, varieties, time and place of growth, more. 2,706 illustrations. xlv + 1,678pp. 8½ × 12¼. 23147-X Cloth. $75.00

DOROTHY AND THE WIZARD IN OZ, L. Frank Baum. Dorothy and the Wizard visit the center of the Earth, where people are vegetables, glass houses grow and Oz characters reappear. Classic sequel to Wizard of Oz. 256pp. 5⅜ × 8. 24714-7 Pa. $4.95

SONGS OF EXPERIENCE: Facsimile Reproduction with 26 Plates in Full Color, William Blake. This facsimile of Blake's original "Illuminated Book" reproduces 26 full-color plates from a rare 1826 edition. Includes "The Tyger," "London," "Holy Thursday," and other immortal poems. 26 color plates. Printed text of poems. 48pp. 5¼ × 7. 24636-1 Pa. $3.50

SONGS OF INNOCENCE, William Blake. The first and most popular of Blake's famous "Illuminated Books," in a facsimile edition reproducing all 31 brightly colored plates. Additional printed text of each poem. 64pp. 5¼ × 7. 22764-2 Pa. $3.50

PRECIOUS STONES, Max Bauer. Classic, thorough study of diamonds, rubies, emeralds, garnets, etc.: physical character, occurrence, properties, use, similar topics. 20 plates, 8 in color. 94 figures. 659pp. 6⅛ × 9¼. 21910-0, 21911-9 Pa., Two-vol. set $15.90

ENCYCLOPEDIA OF VICTORIAN NEEDLEWORK, S. F. A. Caulfeild and Blanche Saward. Full, precise descriptions of stitches, techniques for dozens of needlecrafts—most exhaustive reference of its kind. Over 800 figures. Total of 679pp. 8⅛ × 11. Two volumes. Vol. 1 22800-2 Pa. $11.95 Vol. 2 22801-0 Pa. $11.95

THE MARVELOUS LAND OF OZ, L. Frank Baum. Second Oz book, the Scarecrow and Tin Woodman are back with hero named Tip, Oz magic. 136 illustrations. 287pp. 5⅜ × 8½. 20692-0 Pa. $5.95

WILD FOWL DECOYS, Joel Barber. Basic book on the subject, by foremost authority and collector. Reveals history of decoy making and rigging, place in American culture, different kinds of decoys, how to make them, and how to use them. 140 plates. 156pp. 7⅞ × 10¾. 20011-6 Pa. $8.95

HISTORY OF LACE, Mrs. Bury Palliser. Definitive, profusely illustrated chronicle of lace from earliest times to late 19th century. Laces of Italy, Greece, England, France, Belgium, etc. Landmark of needlework scholarship. 266 illustrations. 672pp. 6⅛ × 9¼. 24742-2 Pa. $14.95

ILLUSTRATED GUIDE TO SHAKER FURNITURE, Robert Meader. All furniture and appurtenances, with much on unknown local styles. 235 photos. 146pp. 9 × 12. 22819-3 Pa. $7.95

WHALE SHIPS AND WHALING: A Pictorial Survey, George Francis Dow. Over 200 vintage engravings, drawings, photographs of barks, brigs, cutters, other vessels. Also harpoons, lances, whaling guns, many other artifacts. Comprehensive text by foremost authority. 207 black-and-white illustrations. 288pp. 6 × 9.
24808-9 Pa. $8.95

THE BERTRAMS, Anthony Trollope. Powerful portrayal of blind self-will and thwarted ambition includes one of Trollope's most heartrending love stories. 497pp. 5⅜ × 8½. 25119-5 Pa. $8.95

ADVENTURES WITH A HAND LENS, Richard Headstrom. Clearly written guide to observing and studying flowers and grasses, fish scales, moth and insect wings, egg cases, buds, feathers, seeds, leaf scars, moss, molds, ferns, common crystals, etc.—all with an ordinary, inexpensive magnifying glass. 209 exact line drawings aid in your discoveries. 220pp. 5⅜ × 8½. 23330-8 Pa. $4.50

RODIN ON ART AND ARTISTS, Auguste Rodin. Great sculptor's candid, wide-ranging comments on meaning of art; great artists; relation of sculpture to poetry, painting, music; philosophy of life, more. 76 superb black-and-white illustrations of Rodin's sculpture, drawings and prints. 119pp. 8⅝ × 11¼. 24487-3 Pa. $6.95

FIFTY CLASSIC FRENCH FILMS, 1912–1982: A Pictorial Record, Anthony Slide. Memorable stills from Grand Illusion, Beauty and the Beast, Hiroshima, Mon Amour, many more. Credits, plot synopses, reviews, etc. 160pp. 8¼ × 11.
25256-6 Pa. $11.95

THE PRINCIPLES OF PSYCHOLOGY, William James. Famous long course complete, unabridged. Stream of thought, time perception, memory, experimental methods; great work decades ahead of its time. 94 figures. 1,391pp. 5⅜ × 8½.
20381-6, 20382-4 Pa., Two-vol. set $19.90

BODIES IN A BOOKSHOP, R. T. Campbell. Challenging mystery of blackmail and murder with ingenious plot and superbly drawn characters. In the best tradition of British suspense fiction. 192pp. 5⅜ × 8½. 24720-1 Pa. $3.95

CALLAS: PORTRAIT OF A PRIMA DONNA, George Jellinek. Renowned commentator on the musical scene chronicles incredible career and life of the most controversial, fascinating, influential operatic personality of our time. 64 black-and-white photographs. 416pp. 5⅜ × 8¼. 25047-4 Pa. $7.95

GEOMETRY, RELATIVITY AND THE FOURTH DIMENSION, Rudolph Rucker. Exposition of fourth dimension, concepts of relativity as Flatland characters continue adventures. Popular, easily followed yet accurate, profound. 141 illustrations. 133pp. 5⅜ × 8½. 23400-2 Pa. $3.50

HOUSEHOLD STORIES BY THE BROTHERS GRIMM, with pictures by Walter Crane. 53 classic stories—Rumpelstiltskin, Rapunzel, Hansel and Gretel, the Fisherman and his Wife, Snow White, Tom Thumb, Sleeping Beauty, Cinderella, and so much more—lavishly illustrated with original 19th century drawings. 114 illustrations. x + 269pp. 5⅜ × 8½. 21080-4 Pa. $4.50

SUNDIALS, Albert Waugh. Far and away the best, most thorough coverage of ideas, mathematics concerned, types, construction, adjusting anywhere. Over 100 illustrations. 230pp. 5⅜ × 8½. 22947-5 Pa. $4.50

PICTURE HISTORY OF THE NORMANDIE: With 190 Illustrations, Frank O. Braynard. Full story of legendary French ocean liner: Art Deco interiors, design innovations, furnishings, celebrities, maiden voyage, tragic fire, much more. Extensive text. 144pp. 8⅜ × 11¾. 25257-4 Pa. $9.95

THE FIRST AMERICAN COOKBOOK: A Facsimile of "American Cookery," 1796, Amelia Simmons. Facsimile of the first American-written cookbook published in the United States contains authentic recipes for colonial favorites—pumpkin pudding, winter squash pudding, spruce beer, Indian slapjacks, and more. Introductory Essay and Glossary of colonial cooking terms. 80pp. 5⅜ × 8½. 24710-4 Pa. $3.50

101 PUZZLES IN THOUGHT AND LOGIC, C. R. Wylie, Jr. Solve murders and robberies, find out which fishermen are liars, how a blind man could possibly identify a color—purely by your own reasoning! 107pp. 5⅜ × 8½. 20367-0 Pa. $2.50

THE BOOK OF WORLD-FAMOUS MUSIC—CLASSICAL, POPULAR AND FOLK, James J. Fuld. Revised and enlarged republication of landmark work in musico-bibliography. Full information about nearly 1,000 songs and compositions including first lines of music and lyrics. New supplement. Index. 800pp. 5⅜ × 8¼. 24857-7 Pa. $14.95

ANTHROPOLOGY AND MODERN LIFE, Franz Boas. Great anthropologist's classic treatise on race and culture. Introduction by Ruth Bunzel. Only inexpensive paperback edition. 255pp. 5⅜ × 8½. 25245-0 Pa. $5.95

THE TALE OF PETER RABBIT, Beatrix Potter. The inimitable Peter's terrifying adventure in Mr. McGregor's garden, with all 27 wonderful, full-color Potter illustrations. 55pp. 4¼ × 5½. (Available in U.S. only) 22827-4 Pa. $1.75

THREE PROPHETIC SCIENCE FICTION NOVELS, H. G. Wells. *When the Sleeper Wakes, A Story of the Days to Come* and *The Time Machine* (full version). 335pp. 5⅜ × 8½. (Available in U.S. only) 20605-X Pa. $5.95

APICIUS COOKERY AND DINING IN IMPERIAL ROME, edited and translated by Joseph Dommers Vehling. Oldest known cookbook in existence offers readers a clear picture of what foods Romans ate, how they prepared them, etc. 49 illustrations. 301pp. 6⅛ × 9¼. 23563-7 Pa. $6.50

SHAKESPEARE LEXICON AND QUOTATION DICTIONARY, Alexander Schmidt. Full definitions, locations, shades of meaning of every word in plays and poems. More than 50,000 exact quotations. 1,485pp. 6½ × 9¼. 22726-X, 22727-8 Pa., Two-vol. set $27.90

THE WORLD'S GREAT SPEECHES, edited by Lewis Copeland and Lawrence W. Lamm. Vast collection of 278 speeches from Greeks to 1970. Powerful and effective models; unique look at history. 842pp. 5⅜ × 8½. 20468-5 Pa. $11.95

CATALOG OF DOVER BOOKS

THE BLUE FAIRY BOOK, Andrew Lang. The first, most famous collection, with many familiar tales: Little Red Riding Hood, Aladdin and the Wonderful Lamp, Puss in Boots, Sleeping Beauty, Hansel and Gretel, Rumpelstiltskin; 37 in all. 138 illustrations. 390pp. 5⅜ × 8½. 21437-0 Pa. $5.95

THE STORY OF THE CHAMPIONS OF THE ROUND TABLE, Howard Pyle. Sir Launcelot, Sir Tristram and Sir Percival in spirited adventures of love and triumph retold in Pyle's inimitable style. 50 drawings, 31 full-page. xviii + 329pp. 6½ × 9¼. 21883-X Pa. $6.95

AUDUBON AND HIS JOURNALS, Maria Audubon. Unmatched two-volume portrait of the great artist, naturalist and author contains his journals, an excellent biography by his granddaughter, expert annotations by the noted ornithologist, Dr. Elliott Coues, and 37 superb illustrations. Total of 1,200pp. 5⅜ × 8.
Vol. I 25143-8 Pa. $8.95
Vol. II 25144-6 Pa. $8.95

GREAT DINOSAUR HUNTERS AND THEIR DISCOVERIES, Edwin H. Colbert. Fascinating, lavishly illustrated chronicle of dinosaur research, 1820's to 1960. Achievements of Cope, Marsh, Brown, Buckland, Mantell, Huxley, many others. 384pp. 5¼ × 8¼. 24701-5 Pa. $6.95

THE TASTEMAKERS, Russell Lynes. Informal, illustrated social history of American taste 1850's–1950's. First popularized categories Highbrow, Lowbrow, Middlebrow. 129 illustrations. New (1979) afterword. 384pp. 6 × 9.
23993-4 Pa. $6.95

DOUBLE CROSS PURPOSES, Ronald A. Knox. A treasure hunt in the Scottish Highlands, an old map, unidentified corpse, surprise discoveries keep reader guessing in this cleverly intricate tale of financial skullduggery. 2 black-and-white maps. 320pp. 5⅜ × 8½. (Available in U.S. only) 25032-6 Pa. $5.95

AUTHENTIC VICTORIAN DECORATION AND ORNAMENTATION IN FULL COLOR: 46 Plates from "Studies in Design," Christopher Dresser. Superb full-color lithographs reproduced from rare original portfolio of a major Victorian designer. 48pp. 9¼ × 12¼. 25083-0 Pa. $7.95

PRIMITIVE ART, Franz Boas. Remains the best text ever prepared on subject, thoroughly discussing Indian, African, Asian, Australian, and, especially, Northern American primitive art. Over 950 illustrations show ceramics, masks, totem poles, weapons, textiles, paintings, much more. 376pp. 5⅜ × 8. 20025-6 Pa. $6.95

SIDELIGHTS ON RELATIVITY, Albert Einstein. Unabridged republication of two lectures delivered by the great physicist in 1920–21. *Ether and Relativity* and *Geometry and Experience*. Elegant ideas in non-mathematical form, accessible to intelligent layman. vi + 56pp. 5⅜ × 8½. 24511-X Pa. $2.95

THE WIT AND HUMOR OF OSCAR WILDE, edited by Alvin Redman. More than 1,000 ripostes, paradoxes, wisecracks: Work is the curse of the drinking classes, I can resist everything except temptation, etc. 258pp. 5⅜ × 8½. 20602-5 Pa. $4.50

ADVENTURES WITH A MICROSCOPE, Richard Headstrom. 59 adventures with clothing fibers, protozoa, ferns and lichens, roots and leaves, much more. 142 illustrations. 232pp. 5⅜ × 8½. 23471-1 Pa. $3.95

PLANTS OF THE BIBLE, Harold N. Moldenke and Alma L. Moldenke. Standard reference to all 230 plants mentioned in Scriptures. Latin name, biblical reference, uses, modern identity, much more. Unsurpassed encyclopedic resource for scholars, botanists, nature lovers, students of Bible. Bibliography. Indexes. 123 black-and-white illustrations. 384pp. 6 × 9. 25069-5 Pa. $8.95

FAMOUS AMERICAN WOMEN: A Biographical Dictionary from Colonial Times to the Present, Robert McHenry, ed. From Pocahontas to Rosa Parks, 1,035 distinguished American women documented in separate biographical entries. Accurate, up-to-date data, numerous categories, spans 400 years. Indices. 493pp. 6½ × 9¼. 24523-3 Pa. $9.95

THE FABULOUS INTERIORS OF THE GREAT OCEAN LINERS IN HISTORIC PHOTOGRAPHS, William H. Miller, Jr. Some 200 superb photographs capture exquisite interiors of world's great "floating palaces"—1890's to 1980's: *Titanic, Ile de France, Queen Elizabeth, United States, Europa*, more. Approx. 200 black-and-white photographs. Captions. Text. Introduction. 160pp. 8⅜ × 11¼. 24756-2 Pa. $9.95

THE GREAT LUXURY LINERS, 1927–1954: A Photographic Record, William H. Miller, Jr. Nostalgic tribute to heyday of ocean liners. 186 photos of Ile de France, Normandie, Leviathan, Queen Elizabeth, United States, many others. Interior and exterior views. Introduction. Captions. 160pp. 9 × 12. 24056-8 Pa. $9.95

A NATURAL HISTORY OF THE DUCKS, John Charles Phillips. Great landmark of ornithology offers complete detailed coverage of nearly 200 species and subspecies of ducks: gadwall, sheldrake, merganser, pintail, many more. 74 full-color plates, 102 black-and-white. Bibliography. Total of 1,920pp. 8⅜ × 11¼. 25141-1, 25142-X Cloth. Two-vol. set $100.00

THE SEAWEED HANDBOOK: An Illustrated Guide to Seaweeds from North Carolina to Canada, Thomas F. Lee. Concise reference covers 78 species. Scientific and common names, habitat, distribution, more. Finding keys for easy identification. 224pp. 5⅜ × 8½. 25215-9 Pa. $5.95

THE TEN BOOKS OF ARCHITECTURE: The 1755 Leoni Edition, Leon Battista Alberti. Rare classic helped introduce the glories of ancient architecture to the Renaissance. 68 black-and-white plates. 336pp. 8⅜ × 11¼. 25239-6 Pa. $14.95

MISS MACKENZIE, Anthony Trollope. Minor masterpieces by Victorian master unmasks many truths about life in 19th-century England. First inexpensive edition in years. 392pp. 5⅜ × 8½. 25201-9 Pa. $7.95

THE RIME OF THE ANCIENT MARINER, Gustave Doré, Samuel Taylor Coleridge. Dramatic engravings considered by many to be his greatest work. The terrifying space of the open sea, the storms and whirlpools of an unknown ocean, the ice of Antarctica, more—all rendered in a powerful, chilling manner. Full text. 38 plates. 77pp. 9¼ × 12. 22305-1 Pa. $4.95

THE EXPEDITIONS OF ZEBULON MONTGOMERY PIKE, Zebulon Montgomery Pike. Fascinating first-hand accounts (1805-6) of exploration of Mississippi River, Indian wars, capture by Spanish dragoons, much more. 1,088pp. 5⅜ × 8½. 25254-X, 25255-8 Pa. Two-vol. set $23.90

A CONCISE HISTORY OF PHOTOGRAPHY: Third Revised Edition, Helmut Gernsheim. Best one-volume history—camera obscura, photochemistry, daguerreotypes, evolution of cameras, film, more. Also artistic aspects—landscape, portraits, fine art, etc. 281 black-and-white photographs. 26 in color. 176pp. 8⅜ × 11¼. 25128-4 Pa. $12.95

THE DORÉ BIBLE ILLUSTRATIONS, Gustave Doré. 241 detailed plates from the Bible: the Creation scenes, Adam and Eve, Flood, Babylon, battle sequences, life of Jesus, etc. Each plate is accompanied by the verses from the King James version of the Bible. 241pp. 9 × 12. 23004-X Pa. $8.95

HUGGER-MUGGER IN THE LOUVRE, Elliot Paul. Second Homer Evans mystery-comedy. Theft at the Louvre involves sleuth in hilarious, madcap caper. "A knockout."—Books. 336pp. 5⅜ × 8½. 25185-3 Pa. $5.95

FLATLAND, E. A. Abbott. Intriguing and enormously popular science-fiction classic explores the complexities of trying to survive as a two-dimensional being in a three-dimensional world. Amusingly illustrated by the author. 16 illustrations. 103pp. 5⅜ × 8½. 20001-9 Pa. $2.25

THE HISTORY OF THE LEWIS AND CLARK EXPEDITION, Meriwether Lewis and William Clark, edited by Elliott Coues. Classic edition of Lewis and Clark's day-by-day journals that later became the basis for U.S. claims to Oregon and the West. Accurate and invaluable geographical, botanical, biological, meteorological and anthropological material. Total of 1,508pp. 5⅜ × 8½. 21268-8, 21269-6, 21270-X Pa. Three-vol. set $25.50

LANGUAGE, TRUTH AND LOGIC, Alfred J. Ayer. Famous, clear introduction to Vienna, Cambridge schools of Logical Positivism. Role of philosophy, elimination of metaphysics, nature of analysis, etc. 160pp. 5⅜ × 8½. (Available in U.S. and Canada only) 20010-8 Pa. $2.95

MATHEMATICS FOR THE NONMATHEMATICIAN, Morris Kline. Detailed, college-level treatment of mathematics in cultural and historical context, with numerous exercises. For liberal arts students. Preface. Recommended Reading Lists. Tables. Index. Numerous black-and-white figures. xvi + 641pp. 5⅜ × 8½. 24823-2 Pa. $11.95

28 SCIENCE FICTION STORIES, H. G. Wells. Novels, *Star Begotten* and *Men Like Gods,* plus 26 short stories: "Empire of the Ants," "A Story of the Stone Age," "The Stolen Bacillus," "In the Abyss," etc. 915pp. 5⅜ × 8½. (Available in U.S. only) 20265-8 Cloth. $10.95

HANDBOOK OF PICTORIAL SYMBOLS, Rudolph Modley. 3,250 signs and symbols, many systems in full; official or heavy commercial use. Arranged by subject. Most in Pictorial Archive series. 143pp. 8⅛ × 11. 23357-X Pa. $5.95

INCIDENTS OF TRAVEL IN YUCATAN, John L. Stephens. Classic (1843) exploration of jungles of Yucatan, looking for evidences of Maya civilization. Travel adventures, Mexican and Indian culture, etc. Total of 669pp. 5⅜ × 8½. 20926-1, 20927-X Pa., Two-vol. set $9.90

DEGAS: An Intimate Portrait, Ambroise Vollard. Charming, anecdotal memoir by famous art dealer of one of the greatest 19th-century French painters. 14 black-and-white illustrations. Introduction by Harold L. Van Doren. 96pp. 5⅜ × 8½.
25131-4 Pa. $3.95

PERSONAL NARRATIVE OF A PILGRIMAGE TO ALMANDINAH AND MECCAH, Richard Burton. Great travel classic by remarkably colorful personality. Burton, disguised as a Moroccan, visited sacred shrines of Islam, narrowly escaping death. 47 illustrations. 959pp. 5⅜ × 8½. 21217-3, 21218-1 Pa., Two-vol. set $17.90

PHRASE AND WORD ORIGINS, A. H. Holt. Entertaining, reliable, modern study of more than 1,200 colorful words, phrases, origins and histories. Much unexpected information. 254pp. 5⅜ × 8½. 20758-7 Pa. $5.95

THE RED THUMB MARK, R. Austin Freeman. In this first Dr. Thorndyke case, the great scientific detective draws fascinating conclusions from the nature of a single fingerprint. Exciting story, authentic science. 320pp. 5⅜ × 8½. (Available in U.S. only) 25210-8 Pa. $5.95

AN EGYPTIAN HIEROGLYPHIC DICTIONARY, E. A. Wallis Budge. Monumental work containing about 25,000 words or terms that occur in texts ranging from 3000 B.C. to 600 A.D. Each entry consists of a transliteration of the word, the word in hieroglyphs, and the meaning in English. 1,314pp. 6⅜ × 10.
23615-3, 23616-1 Pa., Two-vol. set $27.90

THE COMPLEAT STRATEGYST: Being a Primer on the Theory of Games of Strategy, J. D. Williams. Highly entertaining classic describes, with many illustrated examples, how to select best strategies in conflict situations. Prefaces. Appendices. xvi + 268pp. 5⅜ × 8½. 25101-2 Pa. $5.95

THE ROAD TO OZ, L. Frank Baum. Dorothy meets the Shaggy Man, little Button-Bright and the Rainbow's beautiful daughter in this delightful trip to the magical Land of Oz. 272pp. 5⅜ × 8. 25208-6 Pa. $4.95

POINT AND LINE TO PLANE, Wassily Kandinsky. Seminal exposition of role of point, line, other elements in non-objective painting. Essential to understanding 20th-century art. 127 illustrations. 192pp. 6½ × 9¼. 23808-3 Pa. $4.50

LADY ANNA, Anthony Trollope. Moving chronicle of Countess Lovel's bitter struggle to win for herself and daughter Anna their rightful rank and fortune—perhaps at cost of sanity itself. 384pp. 5⅜ × 8½. 24669-8 Pa. $6.95

EGYPTIAN MAGIC, E. A. Wallis Budge. Sums up all that is known about magic in Ancient Egypt: the role of magic in controlling the gods, powerful amulets that warded off evil spirits, scarabs of immortality, use of wax images, formulas and spells, the secret name, much more. 253pp. 5⅜ × 8½. 22681-6 Pa. $4.50

THE DANCE OF SIVA, Ananda Coomaraswamy. Preeminent authority unfolds the vast metaphysic of India: the revelation of her art, conception of the universe, social organization, etc. 27 reproductions of art masterpieces. 192pp. 5⅜ × 8½.
24817-8 Pa. $5.95

CATALOG OF DOVER BOOKS

CHRISTMAS CUSTOMS AND TRADITIONS, Clement A. Miles. Origin, evolution, significance of religious, secular practices. Caroling, gifts, yule logs, much more. Full, scholarly yet fascinating; non-sectarian. 400pp. 5⅜ × 8½.
23354-5 Pa. $6.50

THE HUMAN FIGURE IN MOTION, Eadweard Muybridge. More than 4,500 stopped-action photos, in action series, showing undraped men, women, children jumping, lying down, throwing, sitting, wrestling, carrying, etc. 390pp. 7⅞ × 10⅝.
20204-6 Cloth. $19.95

THE MAN WHO WAS THURSDAY, Gilbert Keith Chesterton. Witty, fast-paced novel about a club of anarchists in turn-of-the-century London. Brilliant social, religious, philosophical speculations. 128pp. 5⅜ × 8½.
25121-7 Pa. $3.95

A CEZANNE SKETCHBOOK: Figures, Portraits, Landscapes and Still Lifes, Paul Cezanne. Great artist experiments with tonal effects, light, mass, other qualities in over 100 drawings. A revealing view of developing master painter, precursor of Cubism. 102 black-and-white illustrations. 144pp. 8¾ × 6⅝.
24790-2 Pa. $5.95

AN ENCYCLOPEDIA OF BATTLES: Accounts of Over 1,560 Battles from 1479 B.C. to the Present, David Eggenberger. Presents essential details of every major battle in recorded history, from the first battle of Megiddo in 1479 B.C. to Grenada in 1984. List of Battle Maps. New Appendix covering the years 1967–1984. Index. 99 illustrations. 544pp. 6½ × 9¼.
24913-1 Pa. $14.95

AN ETYMOLOGICAL DICTIONARY OF MODERN ENGLISH, Ernest Weekley. Richest, fullest work, by foremost British lexicographer. Detailed word histories. Inexhaustible. Total of 856pp. 6½ × 9¼.
21873-2, 21874-0 Pa., Two-vol. set $17.00

WEBSTER'S AMERICAN MILITARY BIOGRAPHIES, edited by Robert McHenry. Over 1,000 figures who shaped 3 centuries of American military history. Detailed biographies of Nathan Hale, Douglas MacArthur, Mary Hallaren, others. Chronologies of engagements, more. Introduction. Addenda. 1,033 entries in alphabetical order. xi + 548pp. 6½ × 9¼. (Available in U.S. only)
24758-9 Pa. $11.95

LIFE IN ANCIENT EGYPT, Adolf Erman. Detailed older account, with much not in more recent books: domestic life, religion, magic, medicine, commerce, and whatever else needed for complete picture. Many illustrations. 597pp. 5⅜ × 8½.
22632-8 Pa. $8.95

HISTORIC COSTUME IN PICTURES, Braun & Schneider. Over 1,450 costumed figures shown, covering a wide variety of peoples: kings, emperors, nobles, priests, servants, soldiers, scholars, townsfolk, peasants, merchants, courtiers, cavaliers, and more. 256pp. 8⅜ × 11¼.
23150-X Pa. $7.95

THE NOTEBOOKS OF LEONARDO DA VINCI, edited by J. P. Richter. Extracts from manuscripts reveal great genius; on painting, sculpture, anatomy, sciences, geography, etc. Both Italian and English. 186 ms. pages reproduced, plus 500 additional drawings, including studies for *Last Supper, Sforza* monument, etc. 860pp. 7⅞ × 10¾. (Available in U.S. only) 22572-0, 22573-9 Pa., Two-vol. set $25.90

THE ART NOUVEAU STYLE BOOK OF ALPHONSE MUCHA: All 72 Plates from "Documents Decoratifs" in Original Color, Alphonse Mucha. Rare copyright-free design portfolio by high priest of Art Nouveau. Jewelry, wallpaper, stained glass, furniture, figure studies, plant and animal motifs, etc. Only complete one-volume edition. 80pp. 9⅜ × 12¼.   24044-4 Pa. $8.95

ANIMALS: 1,419 COPYRIGHT-FREE ILLUSTRATIONS OF MAMMALS, BIRDS, FISH, INSECTS, ETC., edited by Jim Harter. Clear wood engravings present, in extremely lifelike poses, over 1,000 species of animals. One of the most extensive pictorial sourcebooks of its kind. Captions. Index. 284pp. 9 × 12.
23766-4 Pa. $9.95

OBELISTS FLY HIGH, C. Daly King. Masterpiece of American detective fiction, long out of print, involves murder on a 1935 transcontinental flight—"a very thrilling story"—NY Times. Unabridged and unaltered republication of the edition published by William Collins Sons & Co. Ltd., London, 1935. 288pp. 5⅜ × 8½. (Available in U.S. only)   25036-9 Pa. $4.95

VICTORIAN AND EDWARDIAN FASHION: A Photographic Survey, Alison Gernsheim. First fashion history completely illustrated by contemporary photographs. Full text plus 235 photos, 1840–1914, in which many celebrities appear. 240pp. 6½ × 9¼.   24205-6 Pa. $6.00

THE ART OF THE FRENCH ILLUSTRATED BOOK, 1700–1914, Gordon N. Ray. Over 630 superb book illustrations by Fragonard, Delacroix, Daumier, Doré, Grandville, Manet, Mucha, Steinlen, Toulouse-Lautrec and many others. Preface. Introduction. 633 halftones. Indices of artists, authors & titles, binders and provenances. Appendices. Bibliography. 608pp. 8⅜ × 11¼.   25086-5 Pa. $24.95

THE WONDERFUL WIZARD OF OZ, L. Frank Baum. Facsimile in full color of America's finest children's classic. 143 illustrations by W. W. Denslow. 267pp. 5⅜ × 8½.   20691-2 Pa. $5.95

FRONTIERS OF MODERN PHYSICS: New Perspectives on Cosmology, Relativity, Black Holes and Extraterrestrial Intelligence, Tony Rothman, et al. For the intelligent layman. Subjects include: cosmological models of the universe; black holes; the neutrino; the search for extraterrestrial intelligence. Introduction. 46 black-and-white illustrations. 192pp. 5⅜ × 8½.   24587-X Pa. $6.95

THE FRIENDLY STARS, Martha Evans Martin & Donald Howard Menzel. Classic text marshalls the stars together in an engaging, non-technical survey, presenting them as sources of beauty in night sky. 23 illustrations. Foreword. 2 star charts. Index. 147pp. 5⅜ × 8½.   21099-5 Pa. $3.50

FADS AND FALLACIES IN THE NAME OF SCIENCE, Martin Gardner. Fair, witty appraisal of cranks, quacks, and quackeries of science and pseudoscience: hollow earth, Velikovsky, orgone energy, Dianetics, flying saucers, Bridey Murphy, food and medical fads, etc. Revised, expanded In the Name of Science. "A very able and even-tempered presentation."—The New Yorker. 363pp. 5⅜ × 8.
20394-8 Pa. $6.50

ANCIENT EGYPT: ITS CULTURE AND HISTORY, J. E Manchip White. From pre-dynastics through Ptolemies: society, history, political structure, religion, daily life, literature, cultural heritage. 48 plates. 217pp. 5⅜ × 8½.   22548-8 Pa. $4.95

CATALOG OF DOVER BOOKS

SIR HARRY HOTSPUR OF HUMBLETHWAITE, Anthony Trollope. Incisive, unconventional psychological study of a conflict between a wealthy baronet, his idealistic daughter, and their scapegrace cousin. The 1870 novel in its first inexpensive edition in years. 250pp. 5⅜ × 8½. 24953-0 Pa. $5.95

LASERS AND HOLOGRAPHY, Winston E. Kock. Sound introduction to burgeoning field, expanded (1981) for second edition. Wave patterns, coherence, lasers, diffraction, zone plates, properties of holograms, recent advances. 84 illustrations. 160pp. 5⅜ × 8¼. (Except in United Kingdom) 24041-X Pa. $3.50

INTRODUCTION TO ARTIFICIAL INTELLIGENCE: SECOND, EN-LARGED EDITION, Philip C. Jackson, Jr. Comprehensive survey of artificial intelligence—the study of how machines (computers) can be made to act intelligently. Includes introductory and advanced material. Extensive notes updating the main text. 132 black-and-white illustrations. 512pp. 5⅜ × 8½. 24864-X Pa. $8.95

HISTORY OF INDIAN AND INDONESIAN ART, Ananda K. Coomaraswamy. Over 400 illustrations illuminate classic study of Indian art from earliest Harappa finds to early 20th century. Provides philosophical, religious and social insights. 304pp. 6⅜ × 9⅜. 25005-9 Pa. $8.95

THE GOLEM, Gustav Meyrink. Most famous supernatural novel in modern European literature, set in Ghetto of Old Prague around 1890. Compelling story of mystical experiences, strange transformations, profound terror. 13 black-and-white illustrations. 224pp. 5⅜ × 8½. (Available in U.S. only) 25025-3 Pa. $5.95

ARMADALE, Wilkie Collins. Third great mystery novel by the author of *The Woman in White* and *The Moonstone*. Original magazine version with 40 illustrations. 597pp. 5⅜ × 8½. 23429-0 Pa. $9.95

PICTORIAL ENCYCLOPEDIA OF HISTORIC ARCHITECTURAL PLANS, DETAILS AND ELEMENTS: With 1,880 Line Drawings of Arches, Domes, Doorways, Facades, Gables, Windows, etc., John Theodore Haneman. Sourcebook of inspiration for architects, designers, others. Bibliography. Captions. 141pp. 9 × 12. 24605-1 Pa. $6.95

BENCHLEY LOST AND FOUND, Robert Benchley. Finest humor from early 30's, about pet peeves, child psychologists, post office and others. Mostly unavailable elsewhere. 73 illustrations by Peter Arno and others. 183pp. 5⅜ × 8½. 22410-4 Pa. $3.95

ERTÉ GRAPHICS, Erté. Collection of striking color graphics: *Seasons, Alphabet, Numerals, Aces* and *Precious Stones*. 50 plates, including 4 on covers. 48pp. 9⅜ × 12¼. 23580-7 Pa. $6.95

THE JOURNAL OF HENRY D. THOREAU, edited by Bradford Torrey, F. H. Allen. Complete reprinting of 14 volumes, 1837-61, over two million words; the sourcebooks for *Walden*, etc. Definitive. All original sketches, plus 75 photographs. 1,804pp. 8½ × 12¼. 20312-3, 20313-1 Cloth., Two-vol. set $80.00

CASTLES: THEIR CONSTRUCTION AND HISTORY, Sidney Toy. Traces castle development from ancient roots. Nearly 200 photographs and drawings illustrate moats, keeps, baileys, many other features. Caernarvon, Dover Castles, Hadrian's Wall, Tower of London, dozens more. 256pp. 5⅜ × 8¼. 24898-4 Pa. $5.95

CATALOG OF DOVER BOOKS

AMERICAN CLIPPER SHIPS: 1833–1858, Octavius T. Howe & Frederick C. Matthews. Fully-illustrated, encyclopedic review of 352 clipper ships from the period of America's greatest maritime supremacy. Introduction. 109 halftones. 5 black-and-white line illustrations. Index. Total of 928pp. 5⅜ × 8½.
25115-2, 25116-0 Pa., Two-vol. set $17.90

TOWARDS A NEW ARCHITECTURE, Le Corbusier. Pioneering manifesto by great architect, near legendary founder of "International School." Technical and aesthetic theories, views on industry, economics, relation of form to function, "mass-production spirit," much more. Profusely illustrated. Unabridged translation of 13th French edition. Introduction by Frederick Etchells. 320pp. 6⅛ × 9¼. (Available in U.S. only)
25023-7 Pa. $8.95

THE BOOK OF KELLS, edited by Blanche Cirker. Inexpensive collection of 32 full-color, full-page plates from the greatest illuminated manuscript of the Middle Ages, painstakingly reproduced from rare facsimile edition. Publisher's Note. Captions. 32pp. 9⅜ × 12¼.
24345-1 Pa. $4.95

BEST SCIENCE FICTION STORIES OF H. G. WELLS, H. G. Wells. Full novel *The Invisible Man*, plus 17 short stories: "The Crystal Egg," "Aepyornis Island," "The Strange Orchid," etc. 303pp. 5⅜ × 8½. (Available in U.S. only)
21531-8 Pa. $4.95

AMERICAN SAILING SHIPS: Their Plans and History, Charles G. Davis. Photos, construction details of schooners, frigates, clippers, other sailcraft of 18th to early 20th centuries—plus entertaining discourse on design, rigging, nautical lore, much more. 137 black-and-white illustrations. 240pp. 6⅛ × 9¼.
24658-2 Pa. $5.95

ENTERTAINING MATHEMATICAL PUZZLES, Martin Gardner. Selection of author's favorite conundrums involving arithmetic, money, speed, etc., with lively commentary. Complete solutions. 112pp. 5⅜ × 8½.
25211-6 Pa. $2.95

THE WILL TO BELIEVE, HUMAN IMMORTALITY, William James. Two books bound together. Effect of irrational on logical, and arguments for human immortality. 402pp. 5⅜ × 8½.
20291-7 Pa. $7.50

THE HAUNTED MONASTERY and THE CHINESE MAZE MURDERS, Robert Van Gulik. 2 full novels by Van Gulik continue adventures of Judge Dee and his companions. An evil Taoist monastery, seemingly supernatural events; overgrown topiary maze that hides strange crimes. Set in 7th-century China. 27 illustrations. 328pp. 5⅜ × 8½.
23502-5 Pa. $5.95

CELEBRATED CASES OF JUDGE DEE (DEE GOONG AN), translated by Robert Van Gulik. Authentic 18th-century Chinese detective novel; Dee and associates solve three interlocked cases. Led to Van Gulik's own stories with same characters. Extensive introduction. 9 illustrations. 237pp. 5⅜ × 8½.
23337-5 Pa. $4.95

Prices subject to change without notice.

Available at your book dealer or write for free catalog to Dept. GI, Dover Publications, Inc., 31 East 2nd St., Mineola, N.Y. 11501. Dover publishes more than 175 books each year on science, elementary and advanced mathematics, biology, music, art, literary history, social sciences and other areas.